Theologizing Place in Displacement

American Society of Missiology Monograph Series

Series Editor, James R. Krabill

The ASM Monograph Series provides a forum for publishing quality dissertations and studies in the field of missiology. Collaborating with Pickwick Publications—a division of Wipf and Stock Publishers of Eugene, Oregon—the American Society of Missiology selects high quality dissertations and other monographic studies that offer research materials in mission studies for scholars, mission and church leaders, and the academic community at large. The ASM seeks scholarly work for publication in the series that throws light on issues confronting Christian world mission in its cultural, social, historical, biblical, and theological dimensions.

Missiology is an academic field that brings together scholars whose professional training ranges from doctoral-level preparation in areas such as Scripture, history and sociology of religions, anthropology, theology, international relations, interreligious interchange, mission history, inculturation, and church law. The American Society of Missiology, which sponsors this series, is an ecumenical body drawing members from Independent and Ecumenical Protestant, Catholic, Orthodox, and other traditions. Members of the ASM are united by their commitment to reflect on and do scholarly work relating to both mission history and the present-day mission of the church. The ASM Monograph Series aims to publish works of exceptional merit on specialized topics, with particular attention given to work by younger scholars, the dissemination and publication of which is difficult under the economic pressures of standard publishing models.

Persons seeking information about the ASM or the guidelines for having their dissertations considered for publication in the ASM Monograph Series should consult the Society's website—www.asmweb.org.

Members of the ASM Monograph Committe who approved this book are:

Bonnie Sue Lewis, University of Dubuque Theological Seminary
Miriam Charter, Ambrose University, Calgary, Alberta (retired)

RECENTLY PUBLISHED IN THE ASM MONOGRAPH SERIES

Meyers, Megan. *Grazing and Growing: Developing Disciples through Contextualized Worship Arts in Mozambique*

Kim, Enoch Jinsik. *Receptor-Oriented Communication for Hui Muslims in China: With Special Reference to Church Planting*

Lines, Kevin. *Who Do the Ngimurok Say That They Are?: A Phenomenological Study of Turkana Traditional Religious Specialists in Turkana, Kenya*

Theologizing Place in Displacement
Reconciling, Remaking, and Reimagining Place in the Republic of Georgia

By Curtis Elliott

Foreword by Gregg A. Okesson

American Society of Missiology Monograph
Series vol. 36

☙PICKWICK *Publications* · Eugene, Oregon

THEOLOGIZING PLACE IN DISPLACEMENT
Reconciling, Remaking, and Reimagining Place in the Republic of Georgia

American Society of Missiology Monograph Series 36

Copyright © 2018 Curtis Elliott All rights reserved. Except for brief quotations in critical publications or reviews, no part of this book may be reproduced in any manner without prior written permission from the publisher. Write: Permissions, Wipf and Stock Publishers, 199 W. 8th Ave., Suite 3, Eugene, OR 97401.

Pickwick Publications
An Imprint of Wipf and Stock Publishers
199 W. 8th Ave., Suite 3
Eugene, OR 97401

www.wipfandstock.com

PAPERBACK ISBN: 978-1-5326-3475-8
HARDCOVER ISBN: 978-1-5326-3477-2
EBOOK ISBN: 978-1-5326-3476-5

Cataloging-in-Publication data:

Names: Elliott, Curtis, author | Okesson, Gregg A., foreword

Title: Theologizing place in displacement : reconciling, remaking, and reimagining place in the Republic of Georgia / by Curtis Elliott; foreword by Gregg A. Okesson

Description: Eugene, OR : Pickwick Publications, 2018 | American Society of Missiology Monograph Series | Includes bibliographical references and index.

Identifiers: ISBN 978-1-5326-3475-8 (paperback) | ISBN 978-1-5326-3477-2 (hardcover) | ISBN 978-1-5326-3476-5 (ebook)

Subjects: LCSH: Theology—Georgia (Republic). | Sacred Space. | Place (Theology).

Classification: LCC B28.G46 E4 2018 (print) | LCC B28.G46 (ebook)

Manufactured in the U.S.A. 10/15/18

Contents

Figures | vii
Foreword by Gregg A. Okesson | ix
Acknowledgements | xi
Introduction | xiii

1. Methodology | 1
   Eastern Orthodox Theologizing | 2
   Theoretical Background | 5
   Data Collection and Analysis | 10
   Delimitations | 13
   Importance of the Study | 14

2. Displacement in the Georgian Context | 16
   Locating Georgia | 17
   Conflict and Displacement | 26
   Dynamics of Georgian IDPs | 32
   The Need to Understand Religious Aspects of Georgian IDPs | 38

3. Places of Displacement:
   Borders and the Reconciliation of Place | 40
   Background and Context of the Abkhazian Gali Region | 43
   Dynamics of Border Life | 44
   Religious Practice within Contested Spaces | 52
   Strategies of Reconciling Space | 54

4. Places of Displacement:
   Home and the Remaking of Lived Places | 63
   What is Home? | 64
   Home as the Provision of Psychological Fulfillment | 64
   Home as a Place of Abundance | 68

      Remaking Home in Displacement: Establishing Continuity with the Past | 72
      Faith Narratives in Displacement | 74

5   Places of Displacement: Graveyards and Reimagining Place | 83
      Burial Sites: A Place of National and Religious Imagination | 85
      Maintaining Relationship between the Living and the Dead: General features of Georgian Orthodox Views on Death | 88
      Collective Grief: IDPs in Displacement and The Story of Tangizi | 93
      Graveyards: Sites of Remembrance | 96
      Conclusion | 97

6   Theology in the Context of Displacement:
     The Iconic Frame of Borders, Homes, and Graves | 99
      Theologizing the "Iconic" Borderland | 106
      In-Between Homes: An "Iconic" Theology of Home | 110
      Conclusion: The Displaced Gaze | 119

Appendix A: Maps of the Gali Region and of Abkhazia | 123

Appendix B: Life Narrative Interview Questions | 125
      Abkhazia - Life Situation | 125
      Move from Abkhazia/South Ossetia | 125
      Internal Displacement Now | 125
      IDP and Faith | 126

Bibliography | 127
Index | 135

Figures

Map 1. Georgia and Bordering Countries | 19

Map 2. Regions of Georgia | 19

Map 3: The River Ingur (Engur) and Abkhazia. | 28

Map 4: The Administrative Boundary Line and Gali Region | 42

Figure 5: Tavila and her Icon Corner in Tbilisi | 78

Figure 6: Well Maintained Orthodox Gravesite at Stepensminda Cemetery, Kazbegi Georgia. Sept. 2013. | 91

Foreword

PEOPLE ARE ON THE move. In fact, more people are crossing borders now than perhaps at any other time in history. Some of the migration happens quite naturally, with people looking for education, employment, or reuniting with extended families. But some of it takes place unnaturally, with people forced out of their homes and away from all of the things that give their lives meaning. And some of it takes place *within* their countries, leading to what is called Internally Displaced Peoples (IDPs). According to the Internal Displacement Monitoring Center, 31.1 million people were internally displaced in 2016, which amounts to one person every second![1] And by the end of 2016, there were 40.3 million people in the world displaced as a result of conflict and violence. Such movement is quickly redefining our world. It's become a permanent feature of our global landscape.

How do people navigate their identity in the context of displacement? And more specifically, how do religious resources aid them in this process? Curtis Elliott's *Theologizing Place in Displacement* breaks new ground in answering those questions. He studies the context of the Republic of Georgia and the internal displacement of people over the contested Abkhazian region. What makes Elliot's study significant is the focus he provides for how everyday people use religion to navigate the travails of displacement.

Specifically, Elliott examines three places where people theologize upon displacement, borders, homes, and graves. He shows how people navigate the loss of place *through* their Orthodox tradition, and especially through the means of icons. He thus examines each of these places–borders, homes, and graves–through the iconic frame, showing how the

1. Internal Displacement Monitoring Center, http://www.internal-displacement.org/global-report/grid2017/#on-the-grid, accessed August 2, 2017.

Orthodox understanding of icons helps people to re-place, even when living in the context of displacement. This is a theological study of the greatest importance.

Not only does this book contribute to the critical role that religion makes to the study of internal displacement, but Elliott's methodology advances of our understanding of the relationship between sociology and theology. He locates his research at the intersection of ethnography and theology, showing how ethnography foregrounds the voices of grassroots theologizing, and then reveals how the theologizing emanating from the voices of people helps inform sociological realities, such as living in displacement. Hence, the two disciplines need each other, and in complex ways.

This book is a marvelous read. Elliott masterfully tells stories, while intermingling the theological insights emerging from the voices from the ground with robust engagement in the seminal literature. I believe that *Theologizing Place in Displacement* makes a significant contribution to our understanding of what happens to people in the contexts of internal displacement. And this book will become increasingly important as all evidence suggests that people will continue to be forced out of their homes and far away from the places that give their lives meaning. What they do in displacement is a story that needs to be told. And Elliott tells us that story through this book.

Gregg A. Okesson
Dean, E. Stanley Jones School of World Mission and Evangelism
Asbury Theological Seminary
Wilmore, Kentucky

Acknowledgments

No project of this magnitude would be complete without drawing attention to the numerous individuals who helped me shape and ultimately realize its completion. My life was forever changed the year I set foot on Georgian soil, met its hospitable and resilient people, and enjoyed its culture and cuisine. Now some twenty years later, the country of Georgia is still on my mind. This is in part due to my good friend Maya Bibileishvili, who served as my primary translator some seventeen years ago, and who has continued to draw my attention to the plight of Georgian IDPs over these many years. Her work for the Norwegian Refugee Council (NRC), and now for the United Nations in Georgia, continue to help inspire and to shape policy and intervention in that country. Her efforts on my behalf are too numerous to mention. Another friend who was a great help to me in my fieldwork was Ms. Lucy Kvernadze. She sacrificially adapted her work schedule to accompany me on many home visits to IDPs. Her sensitivity and knowledge of local terrain made those days in Tbilisi fruitful and productive. In this same vein, I would like to thank the many IDPs who agreed to share with me their stories of survival and faith. Their courage to endure the many hardships of the last twenty-two years of displacement is truly inspiring and transformative.

I would especially like to acknowledge the Salvation Army, their regional leaders and international leaders who helped encourage me to pursue this topic. I would like to thank Majors Bradley and Anita Caldwell who provided me a spare bedroom and meals during my fieldwork, and a listening ear to the kinds of information I was learning. They, more than anyone else, helped me feel at home and at ease.

Back here in the US, I owe a great deal of respect and gratitude to my friend and colleague Dr. John Erickson, whose generosity both of time and resources allowed this project to succeed. His care for our family during this PhD process was providential, warm, and self-giving, and will shape us as a family for years to come. I would also like to acknowledge my mentor, Dr. Gregg Okesson, whose wisdom and care made this process enjoyable. He was a constant source of encouragement and he continually pushed me to see beyond my own limitations, especially in moments of self-doubt.

Finally, and most importantly, I would like to thank my dear wife Margaret, who means more to me every day, and without whom I would never have dared to venture out into a postgraduate degree. Her love, steady faithfulness, and attention to the details of life during these past years have made our family stronger than ever. To God be the glory!

Introduction

IN THE PRE-DAWN HOURS, approximately one week before war would officially come to her town, Tavila had a dream that would alter the course of her life. In her dream, Tavila found herself in a village near Sokhumi, the capital of Abkhazia, a region within the country of Georgia. The village was one she visited frequently in her early childhood years. The dream recounted a childhood friend's unexpected illness and the final hours of life beside her bed. Before her friend died, she gave Tavila a notebook with four or five pages of names—including family friends or acquaintances—all residents of the village she was visiting. Before her friend died, she whispered to Tavila, "I am waiting for these people in heaven." When Tavila awoke, she felt a sense of fear and dread. As an Orthodox Christian, Tavila believed that when someone dies, they would be waiting in heaven to greet their friends and family members who would die sometime later. Little did she know that her dream was a foreshadowing of things to come. Over the next several weeks and months, Tavila told me that almost 80 percent of the villagers who were listed in her childhood friend's notebook pages would die in a war that no one really wanted. Those who survived, including Tavila, were driven from their homes and displaced to other parts of the country. With tears in her eyes, Tavila said, "This young girl was waiting in heaven for these people . . . she made the list of the people who would die."[1]

Forced displacement has become for many Georgian Orthodox Christians a theologizing experience.[2] This story, and others like it,

---

1. Tavila, interviewed by author, September 30, 2013.
2. Timothy L. Smith first used the phrase "migration is a theologizing experience" in his work on religion and ethnicity in America. See Massey and Higgins, "The Effect of Immigration on Religious Belief and Practice." Massey and Higgins borrow the theologizing concept from Smith's work, *Religion and Ethnicity in America*, 1115–85.

provides a glimpse of the connection of Christian faith to the profound losses people endure during times of war. The loss of relationships and the loss of homes—with their memories, experiences and longed-for-futures would continue to characterize Tavila's life for the next twenty years. Though nearly two decades had passed since she was forced to flee her home, her faith in God would prove to be central in the retelling of her life story. She recounted how God had led her out, protected her, and would provide for her future needs. She spoke of her devotion to God and her devotion to her homeland as if she relied on the experience of both to sustain her in displacement. The ongoing dream of her life was to return to her childhood home, to see it again and to rebuild. She, like most other displaced Georgian's, more commonly referred to as IDPs (internally displaced persons), will never give up hope that one day they will return.

I first met Tavila in a small apartment where she lived in Tbilisi with her husband and daughter. She was an intensely passionate woman whose hospitality and stories of life in Abkhazia captured not only my imagination but also the attention of local and international NGO's. The family had only recently secured enough money through the help of the Red Cross to purchase a home, remodel it, and expand the outside balcony. Having moved in and out of multiple homes over a period of 18 years, she and her family were finally beginning to call the new place home.

Yet despite their new home, Tavila and others are continually reminded of what was lost. Memories of home and life in Abkhazia constitute a daily longed-for experience that contests every attempt at refashioning their present lives. Movies about Abkhazia, songs from childhood, and memories of growing up years shared with other displaced Georgians, all contribute to a deep nostalgia in which their past lives press upon them in the everyday. Furthermore, religious beliefs and practices often sustain the desire to return. A clear example is the Eastern Orthodox tradition during Easter when every family is encouraged to visit the gravesites of deceased relatives and proclaim over the grave, "Christ is Risen!" How could these displaced Georgian's fulfill that obligation when the locations of their gravesites are no longer accessible to them?

This dissertation is about the aftereffects of the loss of place. More specifically, it is about how people remake themselves and their place after profound displacement and the role that Christian faith plays in that process. My time with Tavila and other displaced Georgians mirrors what

Edward Casey describes as a temptation in modern day conversations about where people are from. He says, "We rarely pause to consider how frequently people refer back to a certain place of origin as to an exemplar against which all subsequent places are implicitly to be measured: to their birthplace, their childhood home, or any other place that has had a significant influence on their lives."[3] Casey goes on to say, "to lack a primal place is to be 'homeless' indeed, not only in the literal sense of having no permanently sheltering structure, but also as being without any effective means of orientation in a complex and confusing world."[4]

The disorientation of displacement, and the resources within Christian faith to re-make place are the two central motifs to be explored throughout this dissertation. In order to more fully understand the complexity around which displaced Georgians negotiate their current lives, I explore the dynamics of Christian faith as it is brought to bear upon three places that highlight and reinforce their displacement. Each place will be looked at in separate chapters (3–5) though in many ways they mutually reinforce one another. My goal is that in examining the role of faith in view of these locations (borders, homes and graves) light will be shed on how Christian responses to displacement highlight attempts to theologize a sense of place by reconciling, remaking and reimagining alternate visions of these contested spaces.

In chapter 1, I discuss the theoretical lenses that will inform the work as a whole. I locate this dissertation at the intersection of ethnography and theology seeking to describe a local theologizing process as it unfolds in the disruptive context of displacement. To accomplish this requires the convergence of the idea of place as a model of orientation in and toward the world and the theological insights that Eastern Orthodox theology provide about humanity's relationship to God as it is made manifest in practice. Religious life in displacement is about negotiating one's loss toward a new orientation for place and about seeing old places with new eyes. This process, as I argue, is inherently theological because of the way it connects social, spatial or "placial," and religious imaginaries, many of which converge in and around various themes in Orthodox theology, tradition, and life itself.[5] In chapter 2, I briefly describe the

3. Casey, *Getting Back into Place*, xv.
4. Ibid.
5. I use the term "imaginary" and "imaginaries" from Charles Taylor, who adapts the term from Benedict Anderson, which refers to "the way we collectively imagine ... our social life in the ... world." Or the ways people are able to think about or

context of the country of Georgia including some of its religious history and the current realities of displacement. Much of the current studies done on IDPs relate to their social integration or to the causes of the wars which cause their displacement. However, in a country where 80 percent of the population self-identify as Orthodox Christians, one cannot simply displace religious identity from the discussion. In chapters 3 through 5 I employ ethnography to demonstrate how religious lives and identities are brought to bear upon places of displacement. These places: borders, homes, and graves, are locations that highlight and reinforce displaced realities. Each of these chapters is a self-contained unit that employs a variety of theoretical insights from each topic area in order to gather together a thick description. In chapter 3 on borders, for example, I show through a case study of a Georgian priest how he attempts to reconcile the contested space of the border region through a series of activities and missions. In chapter four on homes, I first seek to identify what home is by using multiple case studies and testimonies of IDPs. I then describe the relationship between home and faith and demonstrate that IDPs remake or renew domestic space with a combination of material and immaterial factors. For instance, Orthodox liturgy plays a crucial role, but so does the way divine agents participate in establishing a new life in displacement. Chapter 5 on gravesites and remembrance of the dead is the last of the ethnographic chapters and seeks to describe ways honoring the dead is reimagined in displacement. Finally, in chapter 6 I build upon the ethnographic chapters by gathering and synthesizing religious descriptions, and relating them to the larger theological emphasis of icons in Orthodox faith and practice. I argue that theologizing in displacement happens through an "iconic frame" that seeks to reconcile borders, remake homes, and reimagine graveyard imaginaries. Doing theology in the iconic frame ultimately views the materialities of displacement with a heavenly lens and establishes theological significance not only for conceptualizing displacement, but IDP responses thereto.

"imagine their social existence, how they fit together with others, how things go on between them and their fellows, the expectations which are normally met, and the deeper normative notions and images which underlie these expectations." See Taylor, *A Secular Age*, 146; 171. Also see Anderson, *Imagined Communities*.

1

Methodology

My intention in this book is to explore a conversation between the ethnographic description of lived Christian practice and the embodied theology that arises from it. Because my inquiry relates to a description of religious practices and their relation to theology, this book then is placed at the intersection between ethnographic methods and theological inquiry and calls on both disciplinary frameworks to feed into and inform one another. As a project, it agrees with how Nicholas Adams and Charles Elliott describe the purpose of theology as that which teaches Christians "how to see with a view toward transformation."[1] In this case, seeing well means that a "thick description" of religious practices applied within and toward sociocultural phenomenon is a helpful part of theological method if for no other reason than that it provides clues to how Christian faith may be applied in the real world and transform it.[2]

Understandably then, my current methodology is rooted in Christian Scharen's and Anna Vigen's conviction that ethnography is a tool for an embodied theology. They claim, "Ethnography is a way to take particularity seriously—to discover truth revealed through embodied habits, relations, practices, narratives, and struggles . . . and as it is joined with a theological sensibility . . . each particular life, situation, or

---

1. Adams and Elliott, "Ethnography," 364.

2. Paul Fiddes's recent work represents another project, which views observation as central to the theological task. See Fiddes, *Seeing the World*, 11.

community is potentially, albeit only partially, revelatory of transcendent or divine truth."[3]

An embodied theology, however particular as it may be, must also engage the larger and more pervasive social milieu of which it is a part. Among contextual theologians, for example, it is common to view the sociocultural phenomenon of migration as a "sign of the times." Because of its pervasive impact upon identity and faith, migration provides a rich source for understanding the human condition as well as a context that highlights the migrant's experience and understanding of God. Migration therefore is more than a social phenomenon experienced by believing Christians around the world; it is also a significant *locus* for theologizing.[4]

Migration and its various manifestations is perhaps the defining feature of late modernity; and to the extent that it intersects lived (embodied) Christianity it calls for an attempt by theologians and missiologists to understand migration theologically as well as to offer a theological reading of migrant faith. For this book, describing and analyzing Christian religious practices within the disruptive context of forced and now protracted displacement demonstrates an example of an embodied contextual theology that views displacement likewise as a "sign of the times" and a source location for theological reflection.[5]

EASTERN ORTHODOX THEOLOGIZING

The terms theology and theologizing as used in this book rely heavily upon the observed liturgical and ritual formulations of Eastern Orthodox faith practices and the theological reflections that arise from those practices. As will be discovered, theological method in the Eastern Christian tradition, also referred to as Orthodox theology, does not primarily refer to a set of propositions or descriptions about God abstractly conceived, although these certainly do exist. Rather, Orthodox theology

---

3. Scharen and Vigen, "Blurring the Boundaries," xviii–xxi. I would add to this list places. Places are sub-locations within a context or culture that have particular significance for shaping human and religious identity.

4. For example, see Lussi "Human Mobility," 50. Other authors employing the same methodology are Cruz, *An Intercultural Theology*, 1n2; and Groody and Campese, *A Promised Land*, 154.

5. I am indebted to Robert Priest's concept of theologizing, which takes seriously human experience in the world. He says, "[A]n inability to speak knowledgeably and truthfully about humans actually hampers one's ability to communicate knowledge of God." Priest, "Experience-Near Theologizing," 180–81.

in the Eastern tradition refers in part to what Hann and Goltz call the sublime nature of Eastern theological thinking or, more specifically, a mystical spirituality that focuses on a "liturgical discourse *of* and *between* God and human beings."[6] Daniel Clendenin says of the Eastern theological paradigm, "Contemplation and vision, not intellection and analysis, characterize the theological task."[7]

Furthermore, as this book demonstrates, theology in the Eastern tradition not only arises from a liturgical discourse between God and humanity but theologizing occurs in key places that facilitate that discourse and that are shaped by the history of faith, the social imagination, and divine encounters in those places. The theologian John Inge in like manner suggests that "places are the seat of relations between God and the world ... [and] are not irrelevant to that relationship but, rather, are integral to divine and human encounter."[8]

What this means for this present analysis is that the religious lives of displaced Orthodox Georgians will primarily be viewed through the lenses of a liturgical discourse of and between God, themselves, and the places of displacement they engage. In other words, their religious responses to displacement constitute attempts at theologizing about place from within an Orthodox religious frame (including the usage of icons, liturgies, rituals, prayers, pilgrimages, etc.). In the final chapter, I will seek to articulate a theological paradigm that illuminates further the way internally displaced persons (IDPs) in Georgia reorient their sense of place through their understanding and experience of God.

As was mentioned briefly above, this book can also be viewed as another example of a growing body of contextual theology of the way theology and migration (another form of displacement) intersects. Two recent monographs with methodological overlap to this project seek to promote theological reflection by featuring case studies of the religious lives of migrant populations. Both works aim to develop a local or contextual theology based upon the careful observation of religious belief and practice and the significance for theological analysis. *An Intercultural Theology of Migration: Pilgrims in the Wilderness* by Gemma Tulud Cruz deals with theology and migration in the context of domestic workers in Asia. Cruz seeks to "forge a path in the dialogue between social sciences

---

6. Hann and Goltz, *Eastern Christians*, 14.

7. Clendenin, *Eastern Orthodox Christianity*, 55.

8. Inge, *A Christian Theology of Place*, 57–58.

and theology, particularly migration studies and in the emerging way of doing theology, that is, intercultural theology."[9] Her overall project seeks to outline the contours of a theology of female Filipino domestic workers in the context of migration and argues for a "feminist theology of struggle."[10]

The second monograph, *Migration and Theology, The Case of Chinese Christian Communities in Hungary and Romania and the Globalisation-Context*, is a work by the anthropologist-theologian Dorottya Nagy. She argues for a renewed concept of the neighbor in biblical/theological sources as a way of conceptualizing the relationship between minority Christian groups (i.e., immigrant churches) within settings where a majority group's historical church continues to dominate the cultural landscape.[11] Both of these works demonstrate the need to understand Christian faith in a situation of displacement as a way of doing theology. In the Asian context, domestic helpers negotiate different layers of their Christian identity with regard to oppressive structures of society. What Cruz calls a "feminist theology of struggle" emerges as Filipino domestic helpers reflect upon their faith in light of these structures. In Eastern Europe, Nagy conducts case studies of the lived faith of a minority Chinese Christian population who negotiates religious identity as outsiders in an already entrenched religious context. In conjunction with this community of practice, she offers a way of looking at neighbor in a more robust theological way.

Each of these works deals directly or indirectly with the concept of place. In Gemma Cruz's work, she speaks of the place of the wilderness as a driving metaphor to describe the pilgrim-like characteristics of economic migrants. Nagy, likewise speaks of the relational space of Christian communities formed by globalization processes as the *loci* "where theologizing on migration takes place."[12] Therefore, in conjunction with the above works, my present methodology will likewise examine religious responses of Orthodox Christians to displacement (through ethnography) as attempts to theologize about their experience of place.

---

9. Cruz, *An Intercultural Theology of Migration*, 326.
10. Ibid.
11. Dorottya Nagy, *Migration and Theology*.
12. Nagy, *Migration and Theology*, 73.

THEORETICAL BACKGROUND

Investigating religious responses to displacement as a process of theologizing requires the confluence of certain theoretical streams that provide illumination and the key assumptions for this project. The first is the concept of place followed by the anthropology and theology of Eastern Christianity.

Place and Displacement

The philosopher of place Edward Casey writes, "To be somewhere is to be in place, and therefore to be subject to its power, to be part of its action, acting on its scene."[13] In the study I will discuss three aspects of place that will be related to the current topic of the religious lives of displaced persons. These include: how places shape human response and relationships, how human agents act on places, and finally how both of these concepts and their interaction can be defined by the term implacement.

According to the philosopher Edward Casey, the power of place, which includes the smallest of locations such as a room or a yard, to the largest of locations including a region or a nation "determines not only *where* I am in a limited sense of cartographic location but *how* I am together with others and even *who* we shall become together."[14] At least two observations from Casey's statement provide entrance into the interpretive framework of the book. First, Casey's definition highlights the power of place to directly determine or influence human activity. One builds or buys a home in this spot rather than that one. A person may return again and again to a certain location (either in actuality or in memory) because of the feeling he/she has when there. Places have the power to gather or hold together important, even sacred, themes or events. A certain place may hold together memories and imaginaries for individuals or whole communities and affect present or future trajectories. Anthropologist Keith Basso suggests that "places possess a marked capacity for triggering acts of self-reflection, inspiring thoughts about who one presently is, or memories of who one used to be, or musings on who one might become."[15] Secondly, Casey's definition links place with relationships and therefore biographies. The power of a place is found in its ubiquitous presence and its ability to connect the human subject to

---

13. Casey, *Getting Back into Place*, 23.
14. Ibid.
15. Basso, *Wisdom Sits in Places*, 107.

something or someone beyond itself. As I will show in this book, places often evoke a historical and biographical relationship with the divine, or a community with itself, especially if that community perceives itself as having a Christian history or a divine origin. Biographies or stories of places cannot be understood without the biographies of the people who live or move in them and their experience of God in those places. The theologian John Inge asserts that a theology *of* place is foundational to Old and New Testament narratives and must be viewed as relational—the dynamic interaction and experience between people, places, and God. He rightly critiques any notion that place is merely an abstraction or an added alongside to the human experience of God.[16]

However, the insistence upon the power of place to influence human experience in these ways must also be held together with Jeff Malpas's insistence on a dialectic or reciprocity between people and places. Humanity acts upon places as much as places have the power to influence human action.[17] While the place itself may be a suitable home sight because of its nearness to a stream or its mountain view, the human activity of clearing the land, building a foundation and landscaping the terrain will inevitably alter the "wild" space into a suitable dwelling reflective of the one creating it. Not only is this true on a subjective level in human experience, but human agency toward place is connected to culture-making and differentiation, built environments, art and architecture, religious practices, and theology. Craig Bartholomew argues for a Christian view of "place-making" in various arenas of life including in the city, the garden, the university, and in the home where the hard work of practicing place-making must be done "along the grain of God's order for creation thereby enhancing the shalom of all creation."[18]

In contexts of profound displacement, both the "place-shaping" and "place-making" processes in the human-place experience are at work in negotiating ones current place in the world. For example, the power of a childhood home animates itself across space and time and yet the one displaced in turn acts upon current domestic space to form it into

---

16. Inge, *A Christian Theology of Place*, 46–47; 78–82. The Eastern Orthodox view will expand Inge's formulation when it incorporates saints and icons into how sacramentality and encounter is experienced.

17. Malpas, *Place and Experience*, 1. Humanity acting responsibly on the environment for example is the subject of environmental ethics.

18. Bartholomew, *Where Mortals Dwell*, 245.

a place that reflects his/her own identities and values.[19] Without attention to human agency, places of the past become overly definitive and deterministic. Overly prioritizing human agency likewise can lead to a denial of the way former or lost places have structured human response. Yet both are needed in understanding displacement. Particularly, it is the interplay between place agencies and human agencies that lead to what Casey calls implacement and becomes the basis upon which negotiating new places occurs.

To "be in place" and to "have a place" is to be what Casey calls "implaced" meaning to have orientation, belonging, and a sense of being home.[20] Being implaced also refers to the ability to navigate, to chart a course and have meaningful movement within the places humans dwell. Implacement for Casey is also way to think of the "built" cultural dimension of human identity including the affiliated historical, social, political, and religious aspects.[21] However, these dimensions of place also have their negative counterparts. Casey reminds the reader, "displacement threatens implacement at every turn . . . and is endemic of the human condition."[22] All that can be said of place has its near opposite in displacement. If a place has the power to define human identity, what happens to identity when one is now removed from that place? If a place gathers together the sacred space of religious tradition, how does removal from those places alter attempts to connect to that sacred space? Thus, when it comes to understanding displaced persons and their religious responses to it, the idea of place and implacement has heuristic value in that it allows for a more in-depth analysis of a local theologizing process.

In view of the above discussion on place and implacement, this book shows that the main trajectory of human experience in displacement is to negotiate the loss of place by attempting to find place again and/or to recover a sense of orientation or place in the world. In the religious realm, this desire to be implaced takes many forms and is not a homogenous or predictable process. During my fieldwork I found that displaced Georgians inevitably talked about the places that defined their experience of displacement and to which religious belief and practice were directed.

19. Basso, *Wisdom Sits in Places*, 107.

20. Casey, *Getting Back Into Place*, 13.

21. Ibid., 33. Also worth noting is Clingerman's, "Interpreting Heaven and Earth," 48, where he argues that God is discovered in the "depth" of emplacement (also spelled implacement).

22. Casey, *Getting Back Into Place*, 34.

8 Theologizing Place in Displacement

These initial findings became the themes that frame the middle core of this book. These locations I have termed the "places of displacement" and consist of borders, homes, and graves. These locations became "place studies" that highlight and reinforce displaced realities yet open up new ways of conceptualizing place. Because of their connection to displacement, these places are contested in nature and are bound up with human identity, ancestral memory, and religious longing. At the same time, displaced Georgians are consumed with seeking to understand, alter, or transform these places in their daily lives and are ultimately seeking implacement again in view of and despite these places. It is the purpose of this book to discover how they are negotiating the loss of these places with religious resources and how these religious resources are attempts at theologizing about place.

Anthropology of Eastern Christianity

Besides the theoretical lens of place, this study engages the emerging discipline of the Anthropology of Christianity and particularly the small but growing literature on an analysis of Eastern Christians.[23] The relationship between religion and society is especially salient in this current study, particularly in terms of investigating "correspondences between cosmic and social orders" and the way these correspondences relate to responses to displacement.[24] One correspondence is the high degree of congruence with secular, national, and religious identities. Agadjanian and Roudometof argue that the evolution of Eastern Orthodoxy over time cannot be understood without reference to the principle of *complimentarity* between secular and religious leadership. Complimentarity is first and foremost born out of Church tradition where "the religious establishment compliments the secular leader in his execution of duties, providing spiritual leadership and exercising moral control upon state authority."[25] The secular leadership, they continue, "is often allowed and expected to play a role in protecting, expanding, and serving the religious institution."[26] This relationship may help illuminate the desire of

---

23. Unlike Protestant or Catholic studies, Eastern Orthodox Christianity has been largely neglected in the anthropological literature. See the introduction by Hann and Goltz, *Eastern Christians*, 4–8.

24. Hann and Goltz, *Eastern Christians*, 5.

25. Roudometof et al., *Eastern Orthodoxy*, 10.

26. Ibid.

displaced Christians to relate the territorial integrity of Georgia's borders within the discourse of common religious history. A second correspondence between social and cosmic orders is symbolized in the intersection of religious practices and theology. Eastern Christianity tackles this relationship in different ways, but in the Georgian context of displacement it occurs through an understanding of the icon in religious imagination.

The icon and its veneration is the vehicle that translates religious practice into theological and spiritual significance and is a necessary background to understanding responses to displacement among Orthodox Christians. The icon's connection to displacement will be explored in each of the following chapters culminating in chapter 6. It is important to understand some of the general features of the theology of icons that help establish its importance in the study. The icon first and foremost is a theological statement about humanity's affinity to God established and maintained by the Incarnation. Hanganu says, "The Orthodox Christian understanding of icons is founded on the premise that the transcendent God can be represented visually in the immanent form of the icon, since his incarnation as human has demonstrated the possibility of combining in one and the same being both divine boundlessness and human delimitation."[27] Secondly, the icon points to the sacredness of materiality (including places) in both local and cosmic dimensions. As it relates to place and creation for example, all creation has a sacred connectivity to God by virtue of divine energies that create and sustain all life.[28] Thus, the icon if "properly" understood and used in daily life "can open up invisible channels by means of which spiritual energies are directed toward the various realms (including contested places) to the benefit of animated and unanimated elements in the cosmos."[29] In the context of the church for example, icons are to be understood as not only a display of transcendent beauty, but is a movement of divine life from the icon to the worshipper. The perspective, says Metropolitan Anastasoios, is from the "person in the picture toward the viewer" and not the other way around.

---

27. Hanganu, "Eastern Christians and Religious Objects," 45.

28. Creation and materiality, however, cannot be identified with the same essence as God in Orthodox theology for that would be idolatry. Instead creation and materiality are products of divine life (or energies) not God's essence. For a good review of the distinction between essence and energies in Orthodox theology, see Meyendorff, *A Study of Gregory Palamas*.

29. Hanganu "Eastern Christians and Religious Objects," 45.

Theologically it is to "grasp that God and the saints come out to greet us as if heaven is already here to enrich our everyday lives."[30]

In popular religious understanding, as Anders Nielsen points out in his study on icons in the Georgian church, icons are considered "person-like agents with whom the human agents can engage in a social exchange."[31] The agencies of the saints depicted in the materiality of icons are manifestations of divine energies, not to be conflated with God's essence in any way, for that that would be idolatrous, but as energies of God's divine goodness and pathways of his presence through faithful servants. As I will show, this agential aspect of icons is a crucial factor in analyzing religious responses to displacement because many displaced Georgians report having encounters with these spiritual agents in a way that alters their life trajectories.

DATA COLLECTION AND ANALYSIS

This study requires a mixed-methods design combining qualitative data with theological methods. The qualitative methods used are outlined below.

Participants

Participants in this study were ethnic Georgians who had been displaced from Abkhazia in the 1992–93 war. The study included a total of 10 participants, 6 male and 4 female; and the sample ranged from 23 to 73 years of age. All participants identified themselves as devout Christians and had lived in multiple places especially in the early years after the war. At the time of the interviews each participant was living in either Tbilisi or Rustavi in collective centers that were designed by the Georgian government to house IDP families.

Instrument

Using a semi-structured interview process, participants were invited to tell their story of displacement through life history interviews. Interview questions covered three primary areas: their experiences of Abkhazia both before and after the war, their experience of life in displacement,

---

30. Athanasios "The Eschata in Our Daily Life," 39.
31. Nielsen, "Icons and Agency," 229.

and their experiences of God throughout the displacement process. (See Appendix B for the interview guide used.)

Procedure

During my fieldwork I recruited participants initially through contacts that I had maintained from earlier years.[32] Once I had established contact with the Orthodox Christian family, I continued to find other interviews by using a snowball sampling technique whereby one individual or family recommends another individual or family to be interviewed. This allowed me to have some degree of credibility to IDPs despite the fact that I was an outsider. Relational authenticity and connection to existing IDPs are highly valued and so I sought to gain entrance into homes through current relationships since I had not been to Tbilisi since 2007. Every interview for this book occurred in the homes of IDPs. Furthermore, since I am not fluent in the Georgian language, an interpreter was used in order to translate Georgian (and sometimes Russian) into English. The conversations were recorded, transcribed, and analyzed.

Analysis

Interviews were analyzed following the principles of Interpretative Phenomenological Analysis (IPA) first developed by Smith, Jarman, and Osborne.[33] IPA methodology is characterized by three main qualities: idiographic, inductive, and investigative. Schweitzer and Steele, who have applied IPA to studies of refugees, believe that the method is best because it is "open to human experience" and "has the capacity to privilege indigenous knowledge," something that other trauma-related psychological methods do not capture.[34] Moreover, IPA helps the researcher broaden out their research findings because of its incremental approach to knowing. Schweitzer and Steele point out, "Delving deeper into the particular takes the researcher closer to the universal in terms of what is shared and

---

32. I have had rather extensive experience in Georgia dating from 1995, and ending with two months of fieldwork in the fall of 2013. I began working with IDP children in 1995 and continued in subsequent visits. Our organization, The Salvation Army, worked ecumenically with the Orthodox Church to address needs for displaced persons and continues to do so.

33. Smith et al., "Doing Interpretative Phenomenological Analysis," 218–40.

34. Schweitzer and Steel, "Researching Refugees," 91.

also what is unique about the experience."[35] This later step was important because it allowed for the move from particular religious practices to more universal descriptions about God and theology in testimonials.

Smith and Osborne describe two approaches to IPA. The first and most basic method is called the idiographic case study approach and this is the one used in this current study. The ideographic case study approach is recommended for exploration and development of in-depth descriptions from a single case or shared themes from up to ten cases.[36] The interviews followed a semi-structured format so that in keeping with the IPA method, both the interviewee and interviewer would be able to "engage in dialogue whereby initial questions are modified in the light of the participants' responses and the investigator is able to probe interesting and important areas which arise."[37] In my subsequent analysis, each case was compared with the others in a coding process which allowed primary themes to emerge from the data. Later, these primary themes—borders, homes, and graves—and their relation to the religious lives of displaced Georgians, became the centers around which further exploration of religious practices as examples of local theologizing were explored.

The themes of borders, homes, and graves were chosen after my fieldwork was conducted for the following reasons: first, they were continuously referred to, either implicitly or explicitly, in the ethnographic record and thereby represent the essential place-descriptors of displacement around which other major concerns are voiced. Secondly, these places provide scenery where religious belief and practice can be viewed clearly both before and during displacement. And third, these places, by virtue of their importance in displacement, were found to be what I refer to as the places of displacement because they were contested and tended to highlight the tensions, dangers, risks, and joys that characterize the displaced experience.

The first theme of "borders" refers to the border region between Georgian and Abkhazian territories, a chaotic space that is a geophysical marker of IDP individual and collective estrangement. The border in many ways is the root issue to be negotiated with regard to IDPs because it situates all other discourses related to displacement including homes and graves. Without the construction of the border region and the

---

35. Ibid., 92.
36. Smith and Osborne, "Interpretative Phenomenological Analysis," 225.
37. Ibid., 57.

restrictions on returns, the other themes would not operate the same way. Due to the border, IDPs cannot return to their homes or the gravesites of their deceased relatives. For most interviewees, the border operated in the background of life and was a despised feature of a frozen political conflict, a scar on the landscape of their homeland. Though it operated in the background, the border was a constant reminder of the war and representative of the separation from their true homes. For others, namely, Father Archil who I deal with in chapter 3, the border region was all that and more. In addition, it was a place that he sought to transform through religious means, a strategy continually fraught with many obstacles and difficulties.

The second theme "homes" was likewise found to be a major location that characterized the displacement experience. The feeling of being without one's true home and the ways IDPs negotiate their home-loss became the basis of chapter 4. Unlike the border region, the idea of home was at all times referenced as a major location where displacement was experienced on a daily basis. In chapter three I discuss the multidimensionality of home including its religious importance and ways that IDPs remake home in new places through the resources of their Orthodox faith.

The final theme that emerged in the interview data was the gravesites of deceased relatives in Abkhazia. As with homes, graves are contested and inaccessible because of the restrictions of the border. Graves are especially important with regard to religious practices during Orthodox Easter and are prime locations against which to understand how Orthodox Christians negotiate the restriction on gravesite obligations. This is the subject matter of chapter 5.

DELIMITATIONS

From the outset, I sought to delimit my study to internally displaced persons in the Republic of Georgia. While there are many places around the world where the study of IDPs could have been done, I limited my study to the small country of Georgia due to my past experience with people there and due to a limited budget.

Since the majority of people in Georgia (over 80 percent) self-identify as Orthodox Christian, I primarily limited my case studies to those who are active members of local Orthodox churches, although some important stories emerged from Protestant friends whose family members are Orthodox.

Another delimitation was the geographic area of study. The majority of the country's IDPs live in the capital city of Tbilisi. Therefore, due to a limited budget and transportation challenges I was not able to go to other cities and regions where IDPs live but primarily focused my efforts in this area. In one case however, the snowball sampling technique led to an IDP who lived in another settlement in a smaller city outside of Tbilisi. These were some of the unexpected challenges and delights of real-time fieldwork interviewing.

IMPORTANCE OF THE STUDY

This research will explain and describe a local theology, viewing religious responses of Georgian Orthodox Christians to their displacement as an *inherently theological process connected to place*. Therefore, ideas of contested places feature large in this study because the places they are now separated from continue to hold significance to them. In current studies on theologies of place for example, attempts to situate a specific group's interests as local theologizing are lacking.[38] This study adds a human element to a topic of study heretofore concerned with historically critical scholarship. To put it another way, this study locates theology much more firmly in the place-world. What J. E. Malpas suggests about people when he says, "without places, beings would be only abstractions," I want to also affirm about theology.[39] Without places, theologies would only be abstractions unrelated to the lived experiences of people.

The significance of the study is in the fact that it intersects with forced migration and theology.[40] While theologies of migration are growing, they tend to focus on the "movement" of migration and the location of this movement within globalization. This study on place seeks to

---

38. The closest attempt to relate Christian faith to displaced realties is Bouma-Prediger and Walsh's work where they argue for a "redemptive homecoming" in a culture of displacement. Their work utilizes stories of everyday people in homeless situations as a way of talking about Christian homecoming. In Bouma-Prediger and Walsh, *Beyond Homelessness*, 313–20.

39. Malpas, *Place and Experience*, 176.

40. Sample works include Campese, "The Irruption of Migrants," 3–32, esp. ibid., 4n4; also Groody and Campese, *A Promised Land*; Pohl, "Biblical Issues in Mission and Migration," 3; Groody, "Crossing the Divide," 638; Cruz, *An Intercultural Theology of Migration*; Nagy, *Migration and Theology*.

address the other dimension of the globalization/localization spectrum, how place in particular can conceptually help explicate a forced migrant's (or displaced person's) experience of and response to estrangement as well as the theologizing implications of how people appropriate theology in contexts of displacement.

This study seeks to give voice to those on the margins of displacement who have labored for many years at "being home." Because much of the world's IDP populations are protracted, meaning they are unsettled/ and or non-integrated for long periods of time, the ways they negotiate their estrangements, multiple displacements, liminality, and impermanence would be significant for those called to minister to this growing group of people.

Finally, the study represents a growing number of attempts to fill the gap in an overlooked dimension of the anthropology of Christianity by looking at Eastern Christians particularly.[41] While many studies have been conducted on displaced Georgian's as internally displaced persons, at the time of fieldwork, nothing had been written on the religious lives of these persons and how religious identity may be a way of coping with the harsh realities of displacement.

---

41. See Hann and Goltz "Introduction, The Other Christianity?," 1–29.

2

Displacement in the Georgian Context

IN JUNE OF 1995, sometime between two and three in the morning, our flight arrived into Tbilisi, Georgia to pitch darkness. There were no runway lights and the airport itself was barely noticeable against the black landscape. As we de-boarded the plane, we noticed our luggage being loaded onto an old Soviet Era dump truck and driven to an unloading dock where we were to eventually claim it. We entered into a dimly lit room of bystanders all clamoring shoulder to shoulder for a view of friends, relatives, or businessmen. Unlike most Western airports, which were characterized by bright lights, taped off sections with lines to follow, signage, and the somewhat intimidating passport control, we entered what seemed to be a chaotic and formless place; no lights, no lines, and little controls.

As most first time visitors to an unknown part of the world, we were unprepared and ignorant, but nevertheless excited with a faith-filled naïveté about what was ahead of us. We had embarked onto the soil of a country that had more than a thousand years of church history yet had just come through one of the most painful experiences of its long life—seventy years of atheistic communism under Soviet rule. The chaos and barely lit experience of the Tbilisi airport was symbolic of the long night of Soviet rule that had just been lifted. There was little light to reveal the way forward and all that remained was feelings of excitement and insecurity.

Although we arrived under the auspices of humanitarian aid work, we did not fully realize the social and political turmoil that had engulfed this small country only a few years earlier and that would continue on for almost twenty years. In the early years of transition from Soviet hegemony, smaller territories within the historically recognized borders of Georgia sought independence and recognition of statehood as a way of asserting ethnicity and pioneering new futures. In 1992 separatist struggles in the region of Abkhazia contributed to the escalation of war and the displacement of over 250,000 Georgians. Sixteen years later, this time over a disputed territory with Russia, the Ossetian war in the summer of 2008 displaced another twenty thousand. All in all, Georgia, with a small population of 4.3 million people, has seen nearly 5 percent of its population, 270,000 people, forced to flee their homes.

This chapter proceeds by setting the stage for further analysis of the religious lives of displaced Georgians by briefly highlighting how religious identities among Orthodox Christians have emerged over time and in response to disruptive influences. Being located at the intersection of rival empires for example shaped the nation in both its capacity to survive, and in the way the religious identity of a people is tied to its geographical and national imagination. Most recently, for example, Communist atheism's campaign against religious faith led to the resurgence and combination of religious identity fused with nation building in Post-Soviet space.[1] Consequently, contemporary displacement stemming from the breakup of the Soviet Union and the Georgian-Abkhazian war has added yet another opportunity to investigate religious identity.

After a brief overview of the country of Georgia including its religious history and demographics, I will cover the history of the Georgian-Abkhazian conflict, the social realities of displacement, and the various ways current displacement affects the lives of Georgians. I will conclude with the assertion that in a predominately Orthodox Christian country, displacement is not simply a social process to be understood and managed without reference to the religious and theological commitments common to many IDPs. As a historically and culturally rooted faith, Christianity's local beliefs and practices hold promise for understanding IDP responses to displacement as well as conceptualizing religious responses to displacement in a theological way.

LOCATING GEORGIA

Before proceeding, a few caveats are in order with regard to this current study. I will primarily approach this project as an ethnographer and

---

1. Hann and Goltz, *Eastern Christians*, 10.

missiologist/theologian wishing to discern a lived theology, present and active in the context of human displacement. As such, the historical material may seem narrow in scope and insufficient in the minds of some readers. This however is intentional if not inevitable due to the particular focus of the study. Secondly, the Caucasus Mountains and its peoples—of which the country of Georgia features largely—are as complex socio-historically as they are geographically. The density of language groups in such a small corner of the world is second only to Indonesia and is presumably due in large part to its terrain and its history. For centuries, historians, travelers, linguists, anthropologists and archeologists have been fascinated and challenged by this part of the world. Moreover, given its crossroads location between Europe and Asia, it has attracted a wide variety of socio-cultural elements from each of its neighbors. A clear example of this variety is contained in the writings of one of Georgia's most beloved poets, Shota Rustaveli. He wrote what is considered Georgia's national poem called *The Knight in the Panther Skin*. The story contains Christian, Arab, and Persian influences and the hero of the story is presented as a romantic figure who is Muslim (not Christian like Rustaveli). From the preface to the translated edition, Marjory Wardrop says this about Rustaveli, "When he wrote his poem, Rustaveli had evidently no violent prejudice for one religion more than another, but was of a critical and eclectic turn of mind, and formed for himself a working philosophy of life, showing Persian and Arabian tendencies, but with so much of Christianity and Neo-Platonism as to bring it near to Occidental minds."[2]

The modern day territory of Georgia is located between Europe and Asia, to the south of Russia and to the north of the Middle East. (See Map 1.) Considered part of Eurasia, Georgia borders the Caucasus mountain range and lies sandwiched between the Black and Caspian Seas. Countries within and surrounding the Caucasus range are typically divided into Northern and Southern regions. The North Caucasus includes Russia and a host of Russian republics that constitute Georgia's immediate neighbors on its northern border. These include: Dagestan, Chechnya, Ingushetia, North Ossetia, Kabardino-Balkaria, and Karachevo-Cherkessia. The South Caucasus countries include Georgia, Armenia, and Azerbaijan, with Turkey lying on its southwestern edge.

---

2. Wardrop, Introduction to *The Knight in the Panther's Skin*, v.

Displacement in the Georgian Context   19

Map 1. Georgia and Bordering Countries

Map 2. Regions of Georgia

Anyone who spends time traveling in Georgia will immediately encounter regional variations in culture, family names, cuisine, climate, and folklore. There are numerous cultural and administrative regions in Georgia including places like Svaneti, Samegrelo, Racha, etc. (see Map 2). Currently, the regions of Abkhazia and South Ossetia are contested and are the locations of two recent wars: the first in Abkhazia in 1992 (of which this book is concerned) and the second in a central region of Georgia known as South Ossetia in 2008. (See Map 2.)

According to the National Statistics Office of Georgia, the 2012 population of Georgia not including Abkhazia was 4,497,600 people.[3] In the 2013 demographic study by the Caucasus Barometer, an annual survey of the countries of the South Caucasus, Orthodox Christianity in Georgia represented 81 percent of the population, Islam 10 percent, the Armenian Apostolic Church 6 percent, and 'other' and 'none' each being 1 percent.[4]

At the Edges of Empires

Georgia's history has largely been shaped by its relationship to the competing forces of larger empires including the Greeks, Romans, Persians, Ottomans, and most recently Soviet Russia. This means that as peoples and later as a nation it has mostly existed in the frontier zones or the peripheries of these larger national, political and religious interests. In the first century AD the whole of Caucasia including Armenia, and the two primary Georgian kingdoms of Kartli-Iberia (modern day Eastern Georgia) and Colchis-Egrisi (western Georgia) became integrated into the Roman province of Pontus.[5] For three centuries "Romans and Parthians (descendants of the Persian empire) fought over the Armenian and Georgian lands that stood between their rival empires."[6] Much of the same historical patterns of assimilation, resistance, and subordination can be claimed for most of Georgian history until the present day, leading Suny to surmise that survival was the loadstar of Georgia's national and political formation.[7]

---

3. "Population," National Statistics Office of Georgia, GeoStat.Ge. http://geostat.ge/?action=page&p_id=1184&lang=eng (accessed March 2014).

4. "RELIGION: Respondent's religion (%)," Caucasus Barometer 2013 Georgia, http://caucasusbarometer.org/en/cb2013ge/RELGION/ (accessed March 2014).

5. Suny, *The Making of the Georgian Nation*, 14.

6. Ibid.

7. Ibid.

Since the current study makes a claim that Christianity plays an important role in understanding responses to the realities of displacement, the historical context of Christian faith in Georgia is essential to grasp the development of a national-Christian identity. Mystery surrounds the exact entrance of Christianity into Georgia. Church tradition claims that the Apostle Andrew first evangelized the eastern coastal regions of the Black Sea in the second century. Ronald Suny points out that Trebizond and Pityus (near the modern day Georgian-Turkish border) were already bishoprics when St. Nino evangelized the monarch of Kartli-Iberia.[8] At the end of the third century when Rome defeated Persia, Georgian and Armenian lands found themselves within the orbit of the Roman Empire. During this period, the monarchs of Armenia and Kartli-Iberia converted to Christianity, declaring it to be the official religion—Armenia was evangelized by St. Gregory the Illuminator and Georgia by St. Nino between 325–330 AD.

Historians of Christianity in Georgia agree that the Georgian nation developed in connection with a Christian identity that was formed in a largely contested environment.[9] The Georgian kingdom's "official conversion" to Christianity for instance led naturally to entangled relationships between political elites and ecclesiastical leadership. With Christianity adopted as the state religion, Georgia became oriented both politically and religiously toward Roman-Byzantium. But because Georgia was also a buffer state between the Roman and Persian empires, Christianity's development or demise was often the result of alliances, or persecutions at the state level and largely due to policies reflecting the tug-o-war of empires seeking political and religious dominance. This meant that when Georgian princes were overthrown, ecclesiastical structures, learning centers, and the development of church literature would often follow suit. Stephen Rapp points out that when invading armies overthrew political structures, the authority and regard of the Georgian church was diminished accordingly and existing churches fell into disrepair or were destroyed.[10] On the other hand, when Georgian princes regained control,

8. Ibid., 21.

9. Allen, *A History of the Georgian People*; Toumanoff, *Studies in Christian Caucasian History*; Lang, *The Georgians*; Suny, *The Making of the Georgian Nation*; and most recently Abashidze, *Witness through Troubled Times*. Also see Irvin's analysis of Eastern churches under Mongolian rule including Georgia in Irvin and Sunquist, *History of the World Christian Movement*, 447–54.

10. Rapp, "Georgian Christianity," 137–55.

consolidated lands, and united Eastern and Western Georgian kingdoms religious uniformity would also follow.

One of the most defining eras of Georgian Christianity would be the history of the Arab conquests of the 7th to 9th centuries. Stephen Rapp comments that a key component of the Arab strategy was the "colonization of Christian Caucasia."[11] As early as the 630s, Arab armies had launched a series of aggressive strategies for conquest of territory on Georgian's southern borders, and by the 640s they managed to occupy the capital of Armenia. Only ten years later, the borders of Georgia were breached by invading Arab armies, and in 654–655, the city of Tbilisi surrendered.[12] The Arab incursion into the South Caucasus resulted at first in a nominal acceptance of Arab supremacy with promises of riches and honor. However, over the proceeding decades, the Arab rulers became even more aggressive. From the 730s until the 860s, Arab campaigns through the Caucasus under commanders such as Marwan ibn Muhammad and Buga "devastated all of Eastern and Western Georgia" killing both church leaders and princes.[13] On one occasion Archil, the *erismtavari*, meaning "head of the people," and the princes David and Constantine Mkheidze, refused to betray Christianity and adopt Islam. They were tortured and killed and later canonized as martyrs.[14]

Interestingly enough, the Arab conquest of the Caucasus benefited the development of the Georgian Church. As a result of Arab influence, there was widespread displacement of "what may have been thousands of religious and secular elites" leading Steven Rapp to conclude that a new "Kartli-in exile" was created.[15] In the crucible of this exile he shows how Georgian Christianity not only survived, but it flourished in the form of monastic institutions. The result was liturgical renewal and a series of now-famous monks whose biographies recounted extensive growth and development of monasticism.[16]

Despite (and because of) the periods of upheaval and flourishing that defined the development of the Georgian nation, a Christian national identity was in the making. One of the most enduring legacies helping to

11. Ibid., 143.
12. Ibid.
13. Zaza Abashidze et al., *Witness through Troubled Times*, 27.
14. Ibid.
15. Rapp, "Georgian Christianity," 144.
16. Ibid., 145.

consolidate this identity was the document *Conversion of Kartli* (then defined as Eastern Georgia) produced sometime in the 7th century and still widely circulated and discussed today. According to Rapp the document preserves many older memories of how Christianity triumphed and became associated with the ethnic term *Kartvelian*.[17] It was also at this time that the hierarchy and leadership of the church became dominated by this same ethnic group and became a 'national' church organized by and for the dominant *Kartvelian ethnie*.[18] What this means for the current discussion is that during times of social and political upheaval, religious identity is often asserted or re-asserted in new ways, galvanizing the imagination of a national faith. This was true in the history of Georgia and it can be seen again in the way displaced Georgians utilize religious resources in responding to the realities of displacement today. In this next section, I will discuss the impact of the Soviet anti-religious policies against the Georgian Orthodox Church in Abkhazia and other parts of Georgia. These stories set the stage for the forms of religious renewal that can be witnessed today among Orthodox believers.

Soviet Religious Policies and Post-Soviet Transitions: Religious Oppression and Renewal

The generations of those displaced from Abkhazia have lived between the eras of Soviet religious repression and the reemergence and revival of the Orthodox Church in the late twentieth and twenty-first centuries.[19] A well-known story that symbolizes the repression of the Georgian Orthodox Church and its believers comes from a period in the 1970's under the supreme Soviet leader Leonid Brezhnev who was in office from 1964 to 1982. At the local level, the Office for Religious Affairs in Georgia was set up to control and regulate Christian worship, constrict the growth of the church, and coerce believers to refrain from Christian gatherings. In 1972, this same office attempted to prevent mass gatherings of Orthodox believers in the then called Abkhazian Autonomous Republic. In his chapter "From Oppression to Rebirth" Sergo Vardosanidze recounts the following:

17. Rapp, "Georgian Christianity," 144.
18. Ibid.
19. In this way, religious changes have generally followed social processes stemming from the collapse of the Soviet Union, the reordering of geopolitical spaces in the Caucasus, and the introduction of democratic reforms in Georgia.

> Measures taken against the monastery of Kamani were particularly appalling. This monastery was famous for its holy well and thousands of the faithful would visit it on feast days for cures from a range of ailments. By way of reaction, religious affairs bureaucrats demanded the local authorities to block the road leading to the monastery and to cut off the supply of holy water. If these measures did not prove to have the desired effect, they threatened to build a pig farm on the site in order to keep people from bathing in the waters.[20]

This story is significant not only because it reveals the kinds of oppression that occurred during the Soviet Era, but more so, because it reveals how deeply a shared Orthodox identity existed in both Georgia and the Abkhazian republics before the breakup of the Soviet Union. In fact there are many shared sites between Georgians and Abkhazians that have existed throughout the long history of this region, including monastic centers such as Kamani and a famous church in Ilory. As I will show in chapter three, this historical unity is the basis of one man's attempt at reconciliation of these two territories.

Other repressive actions by Soviet policies included such things as the substantial taxation of churches leading to forced closure, forbidding schooling to university students who were known to have attended religious services, and even the murder of priests. Anti-religious propaganda pitted religion against progress, and was a "harmful antiquated shibboleth that hindered the spacious edifice of communism."[21] Statistics at the time showed that the Soviets ordered the closure of more than 10,000 churches in Russia and Ukraine; and in Georgia, out of 1,550 religious buildings in 1921, only 48 churches and 80 clergy remained by the mid to late 70s.[22]

Since the country's independence in 1991, the Georgian Orthodox Church has undergone a massive campaign to reopen old churches, build new churches and expand its religious influence in Georgian society. According to Paul Manning, citing the head of the Georgian Orthodox Church, Ilia II, at no other time in Georgian history have so many new churches been built in such a short amount of time.[23] According to the International Charitable Foundation of The Catholicos-Patriarch of all

---

20. Abashidze, *Witness through Troubled Times*, 232.
21. Ibid., 229.
22. Ibid.
23. Manning, "Materiality and Cosmology," 327.

Georgia Ilia II, the Orthodox Church of Georgia, proceeding from its historical calling, "became one of the main pillars and driving forces for the construction of the new Georgian state . . . this has been revealed not only in the religious and ecclesiastical activities, but in all spheres of social, political, and cultural life of the country as well."[24]

A good example of religious renewal in Georgia today is the social and ecclesiastical influence of the leading figure of the Orthodox Church of Georgia, Patriarch Ilia II. According to a 2008 poll published by the Tbilisi-based International Centre on Conflicts and Negotiation, 94.2 percent of Georgians surveyed ranked Ilia II the most trusted man in the country.[25] Another sign of his popular appeal to Georgian society happened in December of 2007. The patriarch announced he would personally baptize newborns in an effort to battle Georgia's declining birthrate. As a result, thousands of people turned up to mass baptisms, during which smiling parents watched as robed priests plunged screaming babies into ornate vats full of holy water. During my fieldwork, several IDP families had pictures of Ilia II baptizing their children on their walls as a reminder. Official statistics show that in 2008, Georgia had its highest number of births in nine years. Ilia II claims partial credit for the surge in births. "I have already baptized about 5,000 children," he said. "Parents decided to give birth to these children because they had a chance to be the patriarch's godchildren."[26]

Corresponding with high levels of trust in religious institutions and figureheads, The Caucasus Research Resource Centers (CRRC) data initiative in 2007 found that Georgian society considered religious practices such as church attendance and prayer as important to their daily lives.[27] Approximately 49 percent surveyed said that religion was "very important" in their lives; 40 percent indicated that they prayed more than once a week and attendance at church during special occasions stood at 49 percent. According to Robia Charles who analyzed the data, these numbers indicate that the "subjective importance of religion is quite high."[28]

24. International Charitable Foundation of the Catholicos-Patriarch of all Georgia Ilia II, http://patriarch.ge/eng/ (accessed April 9, 2014).

25. Ivan Watson, "Patriarch Ilia II. 'Most Trusted Man in Georgia,'" CNN, April 26, 2010, http://edition.cnn.com/2010/WORLD/europe/04/23/georgia.powerful.patriarch.ilia/?hpt=Sbin (accessed Feb 2012).

26. Watson, "Patriarch Ilia II. 'Most Trusted Man in Georgia.'"

27. Charles, *"Religiosity and Trust,"* 27.

28. Ibid.

Furthermore, given the post-Soviet transition away from communist Atheism to a burgeoning of religious and nationalist sentiment within the Georgian Orthodox Church, one can see how Charles can assert that religiosity in Georgia (measured by both trust in religious institutions and religious practice) helps "discredit previous secularization theories which claimed that religion and its importance would diminish."[29]

In concluding this first section it has been shown that religious identity in Georgia has been shaped and renewed in the contested spheres of competing empires, religious persecution, and religious and cultural disruption after independence. Nearly 20 years after independence, growth continues at a steady pace in the Orthodox Church of Georgia with new churches, additional priests, and renewed church infrastructure. The appeal of Orthodoxy to the general population remains high. Though sometimes it is difficult to distinguish religious and cultural loyalties, the overall point is that religious identity remains a key factor in the daily lives of many Georgians. The remainder of this chapter will set the stage for later discussion on religious faith within displacement by discussing the dynamics of displacement in Georgian society.

CONFLICT AND DISPLACEMENT

This section will seek to describe the current situation of displacement in the Republic of Georgia. After a brief overview of the Georgian-Abkhaz war I will articulate the various manifestations of displacement in Georgian society. Over the course of this section, I will use displacement in two interrelated ways. First I will conceptualize displacement as a *macro-level* reality in Georgian society by using three key characteristics drawn from multiple scholarly sources that describe the experience of Georgian's forced from their homes. These three characteristics of displacement are: *internal, multiple, and protracted* and will form the main structure of the remainder of the chapter. Each of these terms originates within the discourses of the international community, including humanitarian, developmental, and governmental agencies, and serve as ways in which to discuss the larger social and political realities of displacement. As important as these descriptors are, they must be understood along with the experiences of displaced persons. I will also utilize these terms

---

29. Ibid. Also see Abashidze, *Witness through Troubled Times*, 241–46, where the authors argue that the growth and influence of the church in society occurred after independence.

to discuss displacement at the micro-level, including its personal and experiential sense of loss or of being out of place—estranged and separated with regard to one's home, birthplace, land, and religious practices. The result of both the macro and micro perspectives reveal that the effect of displacement has served to disrupt and contest the sacred, bounded, and historical homeland imaginary with which the Georgian Orthodox Church and nation sustain their development. Furthermore, displacement has engendered what Peter Kabachnik calls "cartographic anxiety" in Georgian IDPs.[30] The loss of their homes with the loss of Abkhazia has created a real and imagined anxiety among IDPs about the legitimate borders of the Georgian nation and by implication their rightful place in the world. What I hope to show in future chapters is that with the now contested nature of the homeland imaginary, many IDPs consider displacement as a theologizing moment for themselves and the nation.

Georgian-Abkhazian War

On August 14th, 1992, The Georgian National Guard with military tanks and jeeps crossed the Enguri River,[31] a naturally occurring dividing line between Abhazia and Georgia, and made their way to Sokhumi, the capital of Abkhazia, in an effort to dismantle Abkhazian attempts to break away from Georgia. (See Map 3 below) During the Soviet Era and specifically under Joseph Stalin in the 1930's and 1940's, Abkhazia was made an autonomous region within and yet still under the administrative governance of Tbilisi, the Capital of Georgia.

---

30. Kabachnik, "Wounds That Won't Heal," 45.

31. In this project, I will be using the Georgian transliteration of "Enguri" to designate the river between Georgian-controlled territory and Abkhazian-controlled. Other spellings include use of the "I" as in Ingur or Inguri and depends largely upon whether one is using the Abkhazian word or the Georgian one.

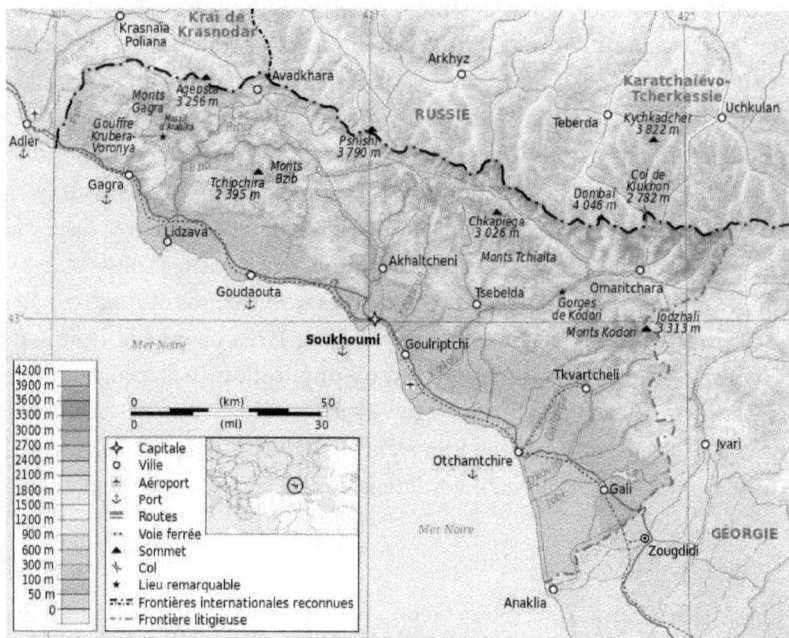

Map 3: The River Ingur (Engur) and Abkhazia.

This development was against the wishes of top-level Abkhazian leadership for it signaled a relationship and image of subordination to Tbilisi. In fact, every ten years or so, Abkhazia would appeal to the Soviet government in Moscow to secede from Georgia in an effort to become its own republic.[32]

During the final years of the Soviet Union until its eventual demise, the winds of change would blow across the Soviet world leading to what Charles King calls the "politics of collapse."[33] This collapse fueled the desire for independence among most of the former Soviet republics, including Abkhazia. The answer for Abkhazian political elites was secession and the attempted redrawing of regional and geo-political maps. Through a series of events and failed political negotiations during the transition years away from Soviet hegemony, Sokhumi's desired secession from Georgia was perceived as a threat to Georgian territorial integrity and the majority Georgian population who lived there. After all, Georgia had come to view Abkhazia as a crucial part of its national borders, especially

---

32. Anderson, *Bread and Ashes*, 195.
33. King, *The Ghost of Freedom*, 212.

since many Georgian's moved to Abkhazia in the 1930's, and many more were born and raised families there.

Failed attempts to win Abkhazia's top leadership over to a future with Georgia eventually led first to small skirmishes and political threats, and then to a full scale military invasion which sought to capture and control Sokhumi. The Georgian military controlled Sokhumi briefly, but the Abkhazians quickly fought back and within a matter of days were able to re-secure the capital. Their strategy mostly consisted of arming rebel groups, hiring North Caucasus mercenaries, and relying upon Russian military intervention, all of which proved effective in pushing back Georgian forces and displacing nearly all of the Georgian population from the region.

Causes of the war are as complex as they are contentiously debated, both in Georgia and Abkhazia, and in the academic community. George Hewitt, Professor of Caucasus Languages at London University's School of Oriental and African Studies lays most of the blame on Georgia for its nationalistic impulses that viewed a potential autonomous Abkhazia as a threat to and a loss of its territorial integrity. He argues that in fact Abkhazia was desirous of better relations with Georgia predicated on a modification of its relationship during the Soviet Era, but that Tbilisi's overtly nationalist policies, simply would not stand for it.[34] Charles King locates the Georgian-Abkhaz war in the larger context of the dismantling of the Soviet empire and lays the blame on "personal ambition, structural incentives, and the simple presence of sufficient quantities of guns."[35] King goes on to say that the conflict did not so much lie in long simmering ethnic hatreds, but in dysfunctional politics stemming from structural features of the Soviet state. Likewise, Cohen and Deng who broadly survey the scope and impact of internal displacement across the globe believe that it is "seldom mere differences of identity based upon ethnic or religious grounds that generate conflict, but the consequences of those differences when it comes to sharing power and distributing the nation's resources and opportunities."[36] The same can be said of the Caucasus context; however, it is no doubt difficult to underestimate the

---

34. Hewitt, *Discordant Neighbours*, 124ff. Hewitt also argues that the war's proximate cause was that Georgian president Edward Shevardnadze started the war in an attempt to gain support for his particular nationalist vision that was under attack by the previous president's political supporters.

35. King, *The Ghost of Freedom*, 211–12.

36. Deng and Cohen, *Masses in Flight*, 21.

power that the collapse of the Soviet Union, whose various institutions and leaders remained gasping for their own breath and viability, had upon the reconfiguration of local, regional, and global politics. While cause may not lie entirely on the doorstep of Soviet policy, it was surely the untangling of the Soviet knot in the Caucuses that conspired to form other entanglements as it unraveled.[37]

Though the Georgian-Abkhaz war lasted only 13 months (August 14th 1992 until September 30th, 1993) the human toll can hardly be overstated. Those forcibly displaced from Abkhazia numbered around 270,000 and most of these displaced would spend the remaining decade in old Soviet hotels and resorts in unsanitary and dilapidated living conditions. It is to these larger issues of displacement both defined within the international community and in Georgia that I will now turn.

Internal Displacement

Human displacement in this small corner of the world was and remains indicative of increasing displacement on a larger scale. A global snapshot reveals that displacement caused by conflict and war represents a growing worldwide phenomenon.[38] Since the late 1980s, the escalation of armed conflict and separatist struggles over territory and national boundaries has contributed to a significant increase in all forms of displacement including refugee flows, forced migrants, and internally displaced persons (IDPs). According to Forced Migration Online, an online database produced in conjunction with Oxford's Refugee Study Center, IDPs far outnumber asylum seekers and refugees worldwide. In 2010, there were 11 million refugees and asylum seekers compared with 27.5 million internally displaced persons.[39]

In a groundbreaking book, *Masses in Flight*, Roberta Cohen and Francis M. Deng aim to "develop a broadly recognized framework of normative standards and institutional arrangements to guide the actions

---

37. For a balanced treatment of the conflict, see Anderson, *Bread and Ashes*, 191–204.

38. Forced Migration Online is a website dedicated to providing access to a diverse range of resources concerning the situation of forced migrants worldwide. See www.forcedmigration.org. (FMO) Also see the International Association For the Study of Forced Migration (IASFM) whose definitions of forced migrants form the basis of FMO's policies and research.

39. "What Is Forced Migration," Forced Migration Online, http://www.forcedmigration.org/about/whatisfm (accessed March 2014).

both of governments and of international humanitarian and development agencies in dealing with the crises of internal displacement."[40] Commissioned by the United Nations and under the academic support of the Brookings Institute, this book is the first attempt to articulate internal displacement and its realities. Early in the second chapter, Cohen and Deng tell the story of the way the term *internal* came to be regarded as a category of human displacement.[41] Essentially, the authors contrast the term refugee with the internally displaced stating that refugees are those who flee outside their country of origin while IDPs remain within their nationally and internationally recognized borders. According to the authors, an increase in internal displacement is evident because the conflicts that precede flight are primarily intra-state conflicts rather than interstate. Conflicts between countries (interstate) have largely decreased since World War II when refugees, asylum seekers, and forced removal of populations required surrounding nations in Europe to deal with masses of people (refugees) moving across their borders.[42] Rather, what occurred in the modern era has been civil wars, failed states like Sudan and Somalia, the Balkan wars, and other internal conflicts that have changed the dynamics of people movements altogether.

According to Cohen and Deng, the international system of aid was developed to address the refugee flows of post war Europe. As such, it created a system of tools, policies and a set of practices to assist those given refugee status. This system however was simply ill equipped to deal with the crises of internal displacement that developed during the last quarter of the twentieth century. The authors site several reasons that internal displacement has become an important topic worthy of policy change and direction. First, there has been a change of outlook by nations that have historically received refugees. These nations near conflicts began scaling back their refugee and asylum policies not wishing to add more vulnerable populations to their own.[43] Secondly, technology and media attention have focused more and more on the plight of those people who are displaced in war and who remain in conflict zones or who move within their own country to set up make-shift refugee camps.[44]

40. Cohen, and Deng, *Masses In Flight*, 7.
41. Ibid., 16–19.
42. Ibid., 12.
43. Ibid., 3.
44. Ibid.

Third, and ironically, IDPs tend to be the most overlooked populations by the international community because they are not privy to aid that is specifically given for refugees. And finally, the IDP plight is often overlooked or neglected by their own governments for various reasons including minority discrimination, political persecution, and a lack of state resources to address humanitarian or development needs.[45]

One of the most important results of the book *Masses in Flight* was the creation of *The Guiding Principles on Internal Displacement*.[46] These principles were first presented to the Commission of Human Rights in 1998 by Francis Deng and subsequently became the standard principles to guide the international community (including NGO's and humanitarian agencies), nations, governments and other actors in providing assistance and protection to IDPs. Based primarily upon international humanitarian ideals, human rights, and refugee laws, these guiding principles cover several important areas: They "identify the rights and guarantees relevant to the protection of the internally displaced in all phases of displacement. They provide protection against arbitrary displacement, offer a basis for protection and assistance during displacement, and set out guarantees for safe return, resettlement and reintegration."[47] These principles offer only guidelines for a general framework of agreement between nations. They do not have the binding weight of law although they reflect and are consistent with international law.

DYNAMICS OF GEORGIAN IDPS

Having discussed the general origins, terminologies, and concepts of internal displacement, I will turn now to the Georgian situation. What follows is an attempt to describe the current shape of displacement and the various attempts to address it, for it is within this general understanding that more specific religious responses will come to have their meanings in later chapters. Keeping this in mind then, for the remainder of this chapter I want to describe broadly the ways displacement is experienced and addressed to give an overall picture of its concerns, realities, and effects.

---

45. Ibid., 71. For a more thorough discussion on the causes of internal displacement, see 19–29.

46. UN High Commissioner for Refugees (UNHCR), *Guiding Principles on Internal Displacement*, 22 July 1998, ADM 1.1,PRL 12.1, PR00/98/109, accessed 13 April 2015, http://www.refworld.org/docid/3c3da07f7.html.

47. Ibid., 5.

Internal Displacement: Between Isolation and Integration

Cohen and Deng point out that in choosing to flee areas of conflict and war, people often remain internal to their national borders because they seek relatively secure and familiar places, including seeking to remain with family members or friends who live in other parts of the country.[48] In the Georgian situation many IDPs relocated to what would eventually become border cities in Georgian controlled territory and others went to family or friends in other parts of Georgia. In a 2012 study done by ABGEO, now renamed Caucasus Peace Forum, researchers explained that the majority of IDPs now live in three main cities of Georgia: Tbilisi, Kutaisi and Zugdidi.[49]

Displacement that is internal highlights a seeming paradox. How can Georgians who have moved to another place within their own country of Georgia remain in a state of displacement for twenty years? In a 2011 study by Conciliation Resources, Magdalena Frichova investigated various attitudes among IDPs including their sense of belonging to society. She found that the majority (83 percent) feel "at ease" in Georgian society.[50] What these statistics don't reveal however is the more complex issue of what it means to integrate into the local population versus remaining isolated.

While many IDPs feel a sense of belonging *as* national Georgians, they may sense marginalization or isolation in other areas such as the lack of economic or educational opportunities, or housing challenges. For example, one integration strategy adopted by the Georgian government and some NGO's has assumed that moving IDPs from dilapidated "collective centers" to private homes would more likely lead to integration. However, as a 2009 study revealed, integration was much more complex than simply moving to newly constructed houses and had more to do with expanding social networks which bridged IDP and non-IDP populations.[51] However, many IDPs remain together either by necessity or by choice and remain relatively isolated from the larger society, but securely integrated within their own networks.

Likewise, economic opportunities or the lack thereof seems to play a role in whether or not an IDP integrates effectively or remains isolated.

---

48. Cohen and Deng, *Masses In Flight*, 29.
49. Khan and Odzelashvili, "A Profile of Conflict," 10–11.
50. Frichova, *Displacement in Georgia*, 9.
51. Mitchneck et al., "'Post'-Conflict Displacement," 1022–32.

A number of projects by Government agencies and NGO's have emphasized economic empowerment through micro-loans and skill-development. The belief was that sustainable livelihoods would most likely lead to IDP integration. Yet employment rates for IDP households remain disproportionately high compared to the non-IDP populations and forces many to remain dependent upon government or NGO subsidies for daily living.[52] Despite efforts to empower IDPs economically, a UNHCR 2009 Gap Analysis indicated that these have been only partially successful due to the lack of information provided, lack of entrepreneurial skills, and the malaise of displacement that has caused many to despair. The reality remains that government and NGO subsidies are often the only forms of sustained income that IDPs have. These allowances, while necessary, have unintended consequences including disdain by the non-IDP population who may also be unemployed, or the stigma associated with registering as an IDP in order to gain the allowance.

What these dynamics suggest is that the idea of being at home is much more complex than residing within your own country. Those who have been forcibly removed from specific landscapes of memory and particular childhood homes struggle with viewing home in other spaces and places. Indeed, the question of integration is difficult to measure among internally displaced Georgian's and despite various reintegration attempts, they largely remain in a state between integration and isolation. The purpose of this study then seeks to address the religious dynamics of living in this "in-between" state without attempting to "solve" the problem of integration. The study seeks to understand how internal displacement is negotiated (not solved) from a religious faith perspective, and how a local theologizing process emerges as a result.

Multiple Displacements: Between Homes

Besides internal, Georgian displacement has also been characterized as multiple. Most IDPs do not live in the same location they fled to after the fighting in Abkhazia. Relocation of IDPs has been primarily driven by the search for durable housing solutions. These solutions range from development and new construction to the renovation of older buildings. Extreme cases too often predominate given the pressure on the government both internally and by international pressure to provide assistance

---

52. Ibid., 1025. Mitchneck cites that 35–45 percent of IDPs are unemployed compared to 15 percent of the non-IDP population.

to IDPs. While admirable, these solutions often create more problems and further the displacement by providing overly simple answers to complex realities.⁵³

One of the most infamous examples of multiple displacement occurred in 2004 when private investment in the famous Hotel Iveria led to the relocation of hundreds of IDP families. Hotel Iveria was once the crown jewel of Soviet era accommodations in Tbilisi. A five star high rise hotel situated in the center of the city and located in 'Republic Square' signaled its dual significance as a symbol of Soviet hegemony over both leisure and city space. Almost overnight, this hotel became a high-rise refugee camp, the first of several homes that IDPs would occupy. For a period of roughly twelve years, (1992–2004) Abkhazian IDPs called Iveria home. Pictures of the hotel during this period reveal certain distinguishing characteristics. Maria Theodorou describes Iveria in the following way:

> Iveria emerged as the highest-profile IDP refuge. The hotel's temporary dwellers had remained in a transition state for eleven years already in 2003. Caught in a limbo state, they were still unable to return home and yet not integrated into the host city; Residents but not citizens. In their prolonged sojourn, IDPs have acted upon the architecture of the building and adapted it to their needs. Balconies turned into rooms. Walls made of wooden planks or blue plastic mark the attempt of the dwellers not only to make home out of a hotel room, but to make this home distinct and personal. Over the years the Iveria has grown into an organic community. As the VIP's of the Soviet Era were substituted by the Abkhazian IDPs, the building's original program was compromised. Life took over and spilled out in what appears as a deformed modernist building.⁵⁴

Despite having made Iveria home for nearly 12 years, the Iveria IDPs became victims in the hands of a countrywide privatization campaign where investors sought to improve dilapidated buildings and failing infrastructure. The result was further displacement.

A more recent example of multiple displacements relates to the ongoing challenge of settling thousands of refugees. The current government

---

53. Elizabeth Cullen Dunn, anthropologist at the University of Indiana, has written about the misplaced solutions by humanitarian aid agencies in the Georgian context. See Dunn, "The Chaos of Humanitarian Aid," 1–23.

54. Manning, "The Hotel/Refugee Camp Iveria," 9.

adopted a state strategy in 2009 to provide housing for all of the IDPs displaced from both Abkhazian and Ossetian wars. At the time of researching for this chapter approximately 45 percent of IDPs had been given homes in 1,600 purpose-built developments. The rest continue to rent, squat, or move from relative to relative. Of those provided housing, many are forced to relocate from the capital city where jobs are available to rural developments where jobs are not. In a 2013 interview with Ramaz Gerliani of the Coalition for Civil Society for Forced Migrants, he reported that, "Some 85 per cent of the refugees assigned housing in [various] regions have returned to the capital since there was nothing for them to live on there . . . When people have managed to find occupations in Tbilisi over the last 18 years, they can't then live on benefits of 22 lari [13 US dollars a month] in a regional settlement, when the minimum subsistence amount is 160 laris."[55] The report concluded by saying, "Many disillusioned IDPs have returned to the buildings that they previously occupied."[56]

Protracted Displacement: Between Settlement and Return

According to the Brookings Institute, most of the world's internally displaced populations remain in a protracted refugee situation, neither able to fully integrate nor able to return to their original homes. Protracted displacement "can be described as a situation in which solutions for IDPs are absent or have failed and IDPs have continuing assistance and protection needs that are linked to their displacement."[57] UNHCR defines protracted displacement as: "One in which refugees find themselves in a long-lasting and intractable state of limbo. Their lives may not be at risk, but their basic rights and essential economic, social and psychological needs remain unfulfilled after years in exile."[58]

The protracted nature of Georgian IDPs is best understood by analyzing the interrelated factors between political, religious, and social tensions that revolve around the concept of an idealized return. On the political front, IDPs have been caught between the state strategy of recovering the lost Abkhazian homeland, and state responsibility of providing immediate protection and solutions to its own populace. No one has

---

55. Gertsmava, "Housing Hopes Dim," lines 26–29.
56. Ibid., line 32.
57. Ferris, *Resolving Internal Displacement*, 61.
58. Mundt and Ferris, "Durable Solutions for IDP's," 3.

argued about this reality more persuasively than Peter Kabachnik, who believes that there is a real connection between the limbo that IDPs feel and the controlling discourse of the state whose policies were aimed at the eventual recovery of lost territory and the reshaping of the Georgian borders to its original form.[59] In his article, he demonstrates the pervasiveness of the territorial integrity narrative in national and societal discourse, and shows how anxiety is produced and disseminated at the loss of territory and in the failed attempts at reconciliation between Tbilisi and Sokhumi (the Administrative Capital of Abkhazia).[60] The government solution forces a conflict between the real and the imaginary. The real day-to-day suffering of many IDPs in harsh living conditions is maintained and reinforced through the political imaginary of territorial integrity, the solution of which is to recover lost land and restore proper borders.

Protracted displacement cannot be explained by political discourse and structural policies of the state alone. In addition, the social and sometimes religious discourses and practices of some IDPs have also been aimed at a persistent commitment to return to Abkhazia that in turn leads to difficulties in integrating meaningfully with non-IDP populations. For example, both Kabachnik and Sulava have researched the phenomenon of "IDP schools," sometimes called "Abkhaz schools in Exile" whose purpose is to educate the generation of IDPs born in displacement about Abkhazia as well as instill a desire to return. These schools were established between 1994–1998 and were originally meant to provide disadvantaged IDP children access to education. Over time they grew in number, at one point to 45, but by 2010 they had been reduced to 14. Sulava says, "School posters depict Georgian-Abkhaz war heroes, beautiful nature and left behind Orthodox churches in Abkhazia. The phrases on posters such as "Remember Abkhazia!" "Remember Your Beautiful Land, It is Ruined Today, But You Restore it Tomorrow!" [These] represent the focus of this educational endeavor."[61]

These schools are places where the collective memory of Abkhazia fuels both current and future IDP imaginaries and those of the next generation. They simultaneously reinforce an IDP identity in displacement

---

59. Kabachnik, "Wounds That Won't Heal," 49–50. Also see Kabachnik, "Shaping Abkhazia," 397–415.

60. Kabachnik, "Wounds That Won't Heal," 47–48.

61. Sulava, *At The Crossroads of Identity*, 25.

and at the same time a mode of estrangement and a sense of being out of place with regard to their current lives.

THE NEED TO UNDERSTAND RELIGIOUS ASPECTS OF GEORGIAN IDPS

Besides looking at political and social factors in responding to displacement, this study specifically asks how and to what extent religious factors play a role in understanding displacement and IDP responses to it. As the story of Tavila in the introduction reveals, and the pictures of Abkhazian churches in the exile schools portray, IDP faith and the underlying beliefs and practices associated with it play a role in how they conceive displacement and how they cope with its estranging and burdensome effects.

Many of the studies and authors referenced throughout this chapter offer a passing reference or a brief acknowledgement of religious realities, but few if any look in depth at how religious identity is brought to bear upon displacement.[62] Sulava's work on the 'Exile Schools' above referenced a poster with pictures of ruined Orthodox churches, but with no explanation as to why this kind of picture is significant. Peter Kabachnik a geographer who uses an interdisciplinary method (anthropological and philosophical) and has done extensive field work with IDPs, has suggested that the desire to see "lost" family members at gravesites is "central to their conceptualizations of home."[63] However his interpretation does not address the religious implications, only offering an explanation that prioritizes the socio-cultural aspects of the importance of family and children.

In perhaps the most extensive collection of life-narratives of current IDPs recorded, Lois and Tamar, compilers of *A Heavy Burden*, introduce their book by linking 'the IDP burden' with the obligations brought about by a reference to religiously inspired tradition. They say:

> The title of this book *A Heavy Burden* comes from the great weight of the war traumas that most narrators reveal. After years of displacement, narrators still need to share with the world their losses and their continuing grief that they could not carry out traditional mourning ceremonies and processes. How

---

62. The only exception to this is Chabukiani's recent article on ancestor worship among IDPs, which may signal a new trend. However, the language of "ancestor worship" is misapplied to an Orthodox setting. The better designation is veneration. See Chabukiani, "Ancestor Worship"

63. Kabachnik et al., "Where and When is Home?," 325.

can you come to terms with your loss if your loved ones cannot be buried next to their ancestors on their own land as tradition requires? It is evidently necessary to address this concern to help people move on with their lives. Unsolved problems of displacement may also cause instability and threaten peace-building efforts.[64]

Lois and Tamar locate the grief of IDPs not simply in war trauma, but in the ongoing loss associated with the inability to practice their religious traditions. Yet, the reader is given no indication that the interviewers placed any priority on understanding these same traditions.

Other studies on Georgian IDPs are conducted by non-governmental organizations, government think tanks, or international relief and development entities like the United Nations and the Norwegian Refugee Council (NRC). These reports tend to focus on issues related to security, human right violations, durable housing solutions, or geopolitical interventions. Yet, despite the energies devoted to understanding, advocating for, and provisioning IDPs, they fail to engage a primary identifier—their religious affiliation. To put it more bluntly, the religious lives of IDPs have been untouched by the academic and development communities; a rather surprising move given that 81 percent of all Georgians identify as Orthodox Christians. All of this points to a serious lack of analysis of the ways in which displacement impacts religious identity including how IDPs mobilize faith resources to respond to and conceptualize their displacement.

In conclusion, the above political, social, and religious factors affecting protracted displacement in Georgia reveal a set of deep estrangements between people and places; home and homeland, and the ways Georgian society attempts to reconcile these "wounds that won't heal." The next three chapters on Borders, Homes, and Graves are places which both highlight and reinforce the displacement experience. These locations emerged as important themes while interviewing IDPs in Georgia. The finding itself is significant for it points to the way places define human experience and vice versa. What I hope to show is that through these contested places, IDPs are theologizing a new sense of place in the world by reconciling, remaking, and reimagining the spaces that they inhabit.

---

64. Losi and Tavartkiladze, *A Heavy Burden*, 8.

3

Places of Displacement

Borders and the Reconciliation of Place

"Gali occupies a constant place in the hearts of those internally displaced persons (IDP) who have had to move elsewhere, which is why there are many things we remember and associate with it. The most painful thing for me in this respect is that I don't live on my land, and I rarely manage to go there at all."

—Mzia, IDP from Gali.[1]

Before Mzia relocated to her current home in the city of Zugdidi, she lived in the region of Gali for a period of five years. Sandwiched geographically between Abkhazia and Georgia, the Gali region is the contested buffer zone known technically as a ceasefire line or the Administrative Border/Boundary Line (ABL). Caught between warring factions of Abkhazian and Georgian soldiers and militia, she lived in the Gali conflict area where she negotiated the harsh realities of border life. To Abkhazians, the border represents a new future of independence; to Georgian IDPs like Mzia, the border symbolizes deep loss and an ongoing suppression of her Georgian identity.

Historically, borders have always been a part of the landscape of the Caucasus. This is in part due to the array of ethnic, religious, and

---

1. Losi and Tavartkiladze, *A Heavy Burden*, 63–71.

geographical divisions that characterize this part of the globe. In fact, borders and boundaries have been significant parts of the changing socio-geographic make up of this "mountain of languages" over the *longue durée* of history. Charles King, an eminent historian of the Caucasus, notes, "Borders, allegiances, and identities have often been on the move. Looking across the entire region, one can see modern nationalisms that barely existed a century ago, long-standing cultural identities that are now nearly extinct, and peoples, languages, and cultures that have appeared, disappeared, and reappeared in a different form."[2]

Borders and boundaries have functioned in the Caucasus for different reasons over time. Some were designed to keep identities and allegiances contained within a particular zone, and others designed to keep them out. However, as King surveys the history of this area, he believes that despite the differences in function, there has been a common characteristic.

> Whether one is a Christian in contradistinction to a Muslim, A Gregorian Christian as opposed to an Orthodox one, a highlander rather than a lowlander, a farmer rather than a nomad, or–often most critically—a person from one clan or village rather than another ... the one thing that is certain is the fact that their [Caucasian] identities were always relational.[3]

This chapter explores some of the relational dynamics of the Administrative Boundary Line with a special emphasis upon the way religious identities and values are brought to bear on life both within and in view of the Gali border region. (See map #4 below) As contested space, the border symbolizes different things to both Georgian and Abkhazian peoples and thus represents a prime setting to describe the way faith is lived out. Future studies are needed on the perspectives of Abkhazians. However, because the Georgian IDPs were forcibly removed from their homes and now negotiate a border region that severs relationships and places of social and religious importance, I have chosen to position the study from their perspective.[4]

2. King, *The Ghost of Freedom*, 14.
3. Ibid., 15.
4. This is not to say that I will show a preference that leads to justification of actions or attitudes of one group over the other. My fieldwork highlighted that despite the highly politicized, even hostile, atmosphere on both sides of the border region, simple acts of Christian love and mercy, and the reconciliatory themes that emerge from these acts, are spread out on both sides and originate from both parties.

42   Theologizing Place in Displacement

Map 4: The Administrative Boundary Line and Gali Region

I will begin by looking at a brief historical sketch of the Gali border region and move quickly into the various types of estrangements that are experienced as a result of the dynamics of the Administrative Border Line (ABL) between Georgia and Abkhazia.[5] I argue that the border politics between Georgia and Abkhazia depersonalizes space by effectively blurring the connections between biographies and places. In this space of ambiguity, religious responses in part seek to bring clarity by transforming space through creating an alternate vision based upon the public display of historically significant images and social memories. These responses are born within the types of identities that Orthodoxy fosters. These responses are attempts at theologizing the renewal and reconciliation of the border space based upon the heroics of local actors, the spiritual role of the church in society, and ultimately the role of the icon in the local imagination.

---

5. See additional maps in Appendix A.

BACKGROUND AND CONTEXT OF THE ABKHAZIAN GALI REGION

Under the Soviet system of government, Abkhazia was set up as an Autonomous Socialist Soviet Republic (ASSR) within the Georgian SSR.[6] The ASSR continued to function until 1991 when the Soviet Union dissolved. The move to create autonomous republics reflected a larger strategy by the Soviets of *korenizatsiia* (indigenization). Indigenization roughly speaking involved two things: the "ethnic categorization of inhabitants and the ethno-territorial division of Soviet space."[7] The implications were enormous. First, it meant a shift in longstanding identities. As Saroyan writes about the Caucasus, "traditional social identities that had been constructed around social categories such as class, clan, tribe, and local patterns of residence gave way, under the Soviet policies, to a newer, overarching identity based on ethnicity."[8] This further meant that the ethnic Abkhaz would be recognized at all levels of the Soviet Administration and the hope was that the policy would serve to win favor with the local populations as well as help solidify the Soviet power base. In addition these new republics would become part of an entire system having access to cultural institutions, administrative positions with the Communist party and a sense of belonging to the Communist state.

The "ethnic consolidation" model that the Soviet Union implemented in Abkhazia and in the Gali region unfortunately set the conditions for rising nationalist sentiment that would emerge decades later. By 1989 the Soviet census indicated that the Georgian population of Abkhazia was approximately 60 percent while the Abkhaz themselves constituted only 20 percent.[9] With the breakup of the Soviet Union, the minority Abkhaz, seeking their own independence from Georgia, set the conditions that eventually led to war and the displacement of the majority Georgian population. With regard to the war's impact on Gali, Weiss says, "As a result of the Georgian-Abkhazian conflict the largest part of the pre-war Georgian population of Abkhazia has been driven out. Apart from single

---

6. The current Administrative Boundary Line separating Georgian controlled territory from Abkhaz controlled territory corresponds roughly to the administrative line set up by the Soviets demarcating the ASSR within the Georgian SSR. The line essentially runs through the bed of the Enguri River.

7. Pelkmans, *Conversion after Socialism*, 9.

8. Ibid.

9. Weiss, "Crossing Conflicting State Boundaries," 217.

individuals, mostly in mixed marriages, the only remaining Georgians in Abkhazia live in the Gali district"[10]

DYNAMICS OF BORDER LIFE

On May 14, 1994, nearly two full years after the initial war broke out, Sokhumi and Tbilisi signed the Agreement On a Ceasefire and Separation of Forces that was later known as the Moscow Agreement. Brokered by Russia and in congruence with the Geneva Peace Process, this agreement provided three important steps for the stability of the region: first, a demilitarized zone in the Gali region with military checkpoints and small and large weapon's restrictions. This zone would eventually be called the Administrative Boundary Line (ABL); secondly, a CIS peacekeeping force[11] made almost entirely of Russian soldiers would monitor the demilitarized zone; and finally, a provision for the safe return of displaced Georgians to the Gali region.[12] Generally speaking, both sides kept this agreement until the next major skirmish in 1998 where Georgian paramilitary forces entered the Gali region and fought with Abkhaz forces. Those displaced Georgians who had returned were again forced to flee the fighting and many of the rebuilt homes were burned by Abkhazian forces.[13]

The Administrative Boundary Line (ABL) runs East-West through the region of Gali and is drawn according to the outline of the Enguri River, a naturally occurring geographic boundary which runs from the Western Caucasus to the Black Sea.[14] The main crossing point between the two regions is the now infamous Enguri Bridge, a military checkpoint guarded by both Abkhaz and Russian soldiers to monitor illegal or un-

---

10. Ibid.

11. CIS stands for the Commonwealth of Independent States, a regional political entity formed after the Soviet breakup comprised of Azerbaijan, Armenia, Belarus, Georgia, Kazakhstan, Kyrgyzstan, Moldova, Russia, Tajikistan, Turkmenistan, Uzbekistan, and Ukraine. See "About Commonwealth of Independent States." CIS, http://www.cisstat.com/eng/cis.htm (accessed January 8 2014).

12. The "Quadripartite Agreement on Voluntary Return of Refugees and Displaced Persons," was signed by Georgia, Abkhazia, Russia and the UNHCR on April 4th, 1994. This Agreement detailed out provisions for the safe and dignified return of IDPs to Gali.

13. Human Rights Watch, *Living in Limbo*, 11.

14. The Enguri River served as a historical boundary marker in the Soviet Era with some slight variation, but was generally viewed as a natural dividing point between Georgian and Abkhazian Republics.

wanted crossings. At the geopolitical level, the Administrative Boundary line, initially a ceasefire line, has turned into the *de facto* eastern border of the Abkhazian nation. Abkhazia's *de facto* status reflects its contested recognition on an international level. Russia as well as a small number of countries including Venezuela, Nicaragua, Nauru, Vanuatu and Tuvalu, are the only countries that recognize Abkhazia's nationhood and independence. From Tbilisi's perspective, and the rest of the international system, Abkhazia is part of Georgia's historical territory and Georgia has a right to reclaim and govern it.

The construction of this border space and the policies surrounding its maintenance point to certain structural and relational dynamics that affect local populations and set the conditions of religious response. The following sections will cover the dynamics of border life as it relates to the consequences of a contested return by Georgian IDPs from the Gali region. This has affected both Georgian-Abkhazian relationships as well as Georgian returnee and non-returnee relationships.

A Contested Return to Gali

One issue that has received much attention among journalists and NGO's has been the provision for a return of the Gali IDPs to Gali and the dynamics of border life that have resulted. As already noted, the Quadripartite Agreement allowed for the voluntary or spontaneous return of the Georgian IDPs to the Gali region, but this return has been far from easy or uncontested by the Abkhaz authorities.

IDPs returning to Gali have led to an increase in studies on the Gali region of Abkhazia in recent years.[15] The Human Rights Watch's report on Georgian returnees represents one of the most detailed works covering politics, security, human rights and other macro perspectives in the region. As the title *Living in Limbo* suggests, despite the agreement for a return of IDPs to the Gali region of Abkhazia, little has been done to comply with the measures that were signed in the Quadripartite Agreement (see footnote 2 above). According to the Human Rights Watch report, the repatriation of IDPs to Gali has followed roughly three movements. The first lasted less than a year (from April to December 1994) and resulted in only 311 persons being resettled. The second "phase" was

---

15. Human Rights Watch, "*Living in Limbo*." More ethnographically relevant works include Weiss's chapter "Crossing conflicting state boundaries"; and Losi and Tavartkiladze, "*A Heavy Burden*."

considered a "spontaneous" return (i.e.voluntary), until 1998 when "renewed violence forced between 30,000 and 40,000 people to flee a second time, destroying infrastructure and about 1,500 homes, including many of those recently rehabilitated with donor assistance."[16] And finally, the last movement, also spontaneous or voluntary has occurred off and on for the last 15 years.

The Quadripartite Agreement implied that the ABL would function like a porous border—where Georgians could travel back and forth from Abkhaz-controlled territory to Georgian-controlled territory. As a porous and contested border, it has developed into an area where suspicion by both Tbilisi and Sokhumi run high. Both parties view each other as attempting to take advantage of a destabilized situation wherein illicit activity including arms smuggling, small-scale skirmishes, and kidnappings are common; all of which impact local populations. Some Georgians have remained and/or resettled, but the majority of the population consists of seasonal migrants going back and forth across the ceasefire line to visit relatives, attend funerals, take care of crops, attend school or receive medical attention.

Faces of Conflict: Georgian and Abkhazian Relations

Borders not only divide one territory from the other, they may also divide longstanding relationships by fostering an environment of fear and mistrust. Later in this chapter, I will examine specific religious practices brought to bear on the circumstances and relationships described in the following paragraphs.

Despite the agreement between the Abkhaz government to allow a spontaneous return of Georgian IDPs, the Gali border region is characterized by hostility and aggression between groups. The following testimony by a Georgian IDP, drawn from *A Heavy Burden*, illustrates this:

> I was born in Abkhazia, in Gali district, in the village of Khomushkuri—it is such a small village. The people who lived there were very friendly, they loved each other very much and now each time I arrive there, my heart hurts [long silence]. There has been destruction, but I worry not so much about buildings being destroyed, but because the relationships between people have changed so much. I would say that our village is empty now. There are a few people, but those who remain there are, for some

---

16. Human Rights Watch, *Living in Limbo*, 16.

reason, very hostile and aggressive towards each other. I do not know why distrust and fear rule. People are even afraid to leave their house in the evening. They are afraid of their neighbors and in most cases they are afraid of each other. Georgians are afraid that someone will see them with Abkhazians, that they will say something about them. The same goes for the other side . . . They are afraid that Abkhazians will see how they are communicating with Georgians . . . In both cases there is some risk. I saw such absolutely different attitudes [among people] that it was hard to believe I was in my native village.[17]

The mistrust among former neighbors stemmed from at least two dynamics: First, mistrust was engendered by suspicion that stemmed from the structural changes in the politics of the region. From the Abkhazian perspective, the search for Abkhazian political independence from Georgia and their desire for regional and international recognition as a territory contested historic relational identities leading to an "us and them" division. Now, the Abkhazian's were the new power brokers on their own territory. One example of how these structural policies have affected once normal relations is underscored by Engurdaleuli, who describes below the relational dynamics that have changed since the time of the war:

[My family] have contacts with the Abkhazians, but these contacts are based on vertical relationships—it's like the relationship between a master and his servant. To survive, we have to toady to them so that they don't treat us badly. In Abkhazia there is no law and there's no authority that enforces the law. Everyone does whatever they like. In short, it's a Mafia system. It's a master and vassal relationship. However, it's been worse in the past. Now it's not so bad, at least people are not killed or injured on a mass scale. We are treated like slaves but [at least] the situation is stable compared to earlier times. There is peace, which is better than war.[18]

From Tbilisi's perspective, the Abkhazian government's search for independence was a threat to territorial integrity while any action by Tbilisi since the ceasefire was seen as a subversive attempt to regain control. The result was that the perceived threat of Tbilisi undermining Abkhazian authority contributed to a newly politicized ethno-nationalism that

---

17. Teah testimony in Losi, and Tavartkiladze, *A Heavy Burden*, 27–31.
18. Engurdaleuli, testimony in Lois and Tavartkiladze, *A Heavy Burden*, 44.

tended to undermine good will in social relationships and pitted neighbor against neighbor.

A second factor influencing fear and mistrust is simply the traumatic experiences of the local population who attempted escape or tried to remain in the contested region during the war. During the height of the conflict and in ensuing skirmishes, many Abkhazian men threatened Georgians and burglarized their homes. Engurdaleuli, an IDP from the Gali region retells a story that happened to him while he was in his home.

> It was an ordinary evening. My whole family was at home watching television. Suddenly we heard a loud knock on the door. My father opened the door. I was in the front room and couldn't see what was happening in the back room. When I heard some noise, I opened the door. I saw someone hit my father on his head with a gun. I didn't even realize it was an armed burglary. My father fell down, later it turned out that his teeth had been broken as well. Suddenly the front door opened and two men in masks came into the room. They grabbed my mother. Then one of them looked into the other room. I instinctively raised my hands. Suddenly, actually in a matter of seconds, he kicked me. It all happened very quickly, in a matter of a hundredth of a second. I fell on my knees, and to be frank, I was so nervous that I don't remember what happened next.[19]

Sadly, this scenario was repeated in many other villages during the war. The IDP cited at the beginning of this chapter remembers that a group of Abkhazian men who called themselves "The Scorpions" robbed her home 58 times over the course of 5 years. Each time, Mzia and her family would hide in the woods behind their home when they heard them coming. Engurdaleuli and Mzia's stories are not uncommon; other families report similar events and the accumulated effect among local residents has resulted in traumatic memories and an environment of fear.

According to Low and Lawrence-Zuniga the nature of contested spaces is that they concretize in a particular site, "unexamined social frameworks that structure practice."[20] As seen in the above testimony, relational dynamics are often the result of tainted social perceptions of one group toward the other that mirror larger social and political structural changes. The Abkhazian drive for independence against its rival Tbilisi had worked its way down into social relationships where ordinary

---

19. Ibid., 46.
20. Low and Lawrence-Zúñiga, *The Anthropology of Space and Place*, 18.

Abkhazian's now exercised a feudal-type system of social hierarchy over their Georgian neighbors. Later I will attempt to show one priest's attempt to reframe these social dynamics through religious practices and historical imaginaries.

The Split between Georgian IDPs and Georgian "returnees"

Complicating matters for Georgian IDPs are other structural changes and policies that the Abkhaz government has put into place regarding the Gali region. The larger political picture adds confusion to the already vulnerable identities of IDPs. While the Abkhaz government has allowed a spontaneous return, they contribute to the non-integration of these returnees by policies that erect barriers to their resettlement. For example, a policy by the Abkhaz authorities has structured society in a way that causes hardship for most Georgian returnees to obtain proper identity documents. Without an Abkhazian passport one cannot buy, sell or transfer property and the only way to obtain one is through a long and difficult process of renouncing Georgian citizenship and filing other documents at the central offices in Gali and Sokhumi.[21]

Despite the hurdles to obtaining the rights and privileges of an Abkhaz passport, many 'returnees' do obtain these identity documents but suffer discrimination and further disillusionment from other non-returnees as a result. In practice, this means that Georgian's who return to Gali are pitted against those who have decided to stay in Georgian controlled territory. Engurdaleuli goes on to say,

> The relationship between the returnees and the displaced is like that of [people from] two different worlds. The world where the returnees live is one of obedience to the rules there. They have the attitude of slaves towards life generally. Those who are on this [Georgian controlled] side are like the rebels, because there's more freedom here. This difference can be discerned between those who have moved here and those who have stayed there.[22]

The results of living in two different worlds have led to a returnee/non-returnee split. Georgian IDPs who have not sought any kind of return to Gali consider those who have as traitors to the cause of a national return. As Magdalena Frichova states it, "Many on the Georgian side of the divide . . . consider Gali returnees as traitors: they have returned to

---

21. For a good overview, see Human Rights Watch, *Living in Limbo*, 31–57.
22. Engurdaleuli testimony, *A Heavy Burden*, 45.

homes under Abkhaz administration, hence are not actively against the Abkhaz independence cause."[23] These factors lead this author to identify the minority population in the Gali region as having a "bifurcated identity" and a "tragic illustration of how vulnerable and manipulated minorities can become in a situation of ongoing conflict."[24]

Gali: Blurring the Connection Between Biographies and Place

The implications of contested places and the way they structure relationships are significant for thinking about people and their places of origin. The relational changes observed above are concretized through the erection and maintenance of the border. And as philosophers of place have pointed out, place has the "power to memorialize and identify us, to tell us who and what we are in terms of where we are and where we are not."[25] The power of contested places like a border region has a similar effect in the opposite direction because it redefines who is 'local' and who is not, who is "in" and who is not. This is all the more acute for those returnees who have sought entrance back into their homes and lands and now find themselves strangers. The social imaginary of what home was has betrayed them as they now return under someone else's rules to someone else's region and must abide by the relational dynamics that are determined by someone else.

In such places, people's historical connection to towns, homes, landscapes, and historical relations are in danger of being erased or at least blurred, so that one's definition of "local" no longer applies. Engurdaleuli says,

> Often when we go to Abkhazia those who live there say that the Zugdidians have come.[26] Once, my relative and I had an argument because of this. We were sitting at the table and they referred to us as Zugdidians. We contradicted them. Why Zugdidians? We were born here [in Abkhazia] and we're locals. Why should they have said that? There must be a reason for this, but I don't know why they did so. It's the same thing here. When we're

---

23. Frichova, "Participation of Persons," 649.
24. Ibid.
25. Casey, *Getting Back into Place*, xv.
26. Zugdidi is one of the main cities on the Georgian territory before one crosses the ABL.

here they refer to us as Galians. It's then that you feel split in two
... It often happens. I've heard that from many people[27]

The experience above signals a new kind of local. Local is no longer defined by the geography of one's birth home or growing up years, and certainly not by one's extended family presence as is symbolized by Georgian IDP grave yards scattered around Abkhazia and the Gali region. Now, peoples' lives and histories, i.e. their biographies, are attached to impersonal cities like Zugdidi, cities that in large part have been re-defined as places-holders for thousands of IDPs, but typically have no personal or historical value as a place.

A very recent example of the separation between people and place occurred during my fieldwork. In September 2013, while I was traveling to a series of IDP camps, Russian military peacekeepers were constructing fence-borders through the village of Ditsi in South Ossetia only twenty kilometers from where we were.[28] The situation was tense and Georgian border guards would only allow us to drive through the camp under close scrutiny. While South Ossetia is a different region from Abkhazia, it remains within the internationally recognized boundaries of Georgia and the social and political situations are similar to Abkhazia. The fence-borders were constructed in a seemingly arbitrary fashion with disastrous results for local populations. Not only were villagers separated from their homes, but portions of these fence-borders were built *between* homes and family gravesites, adding to the tension. The arbitrarily constructed fence-border was a tangible and symbolic dividing line severing ties between personal histories and national geographies. Years of cultivating the connection between biographies and places would now be deconstructed in a matter of days rendering that place contested and no longer personal.[29]

So far I have covered the effect of a contested border region on relationships and upon definitions of locality. The common effect of both of these dynamics leads us back to the ending of the quote above wherein one IDP says, "It was hard to believe that I was in my native village." While this statement is certainly one of shock, it can also signal deeper

27. Engurdaleuli testimony. *A Heavy Burden*, 45.

28. South Ossetia is another contested region that now seeks independence from Tbilisi and has sought Russian protection.

29. Elizabeth Owen, "Georgia: Fence-Fight," lines 1–8. Also see Pelkman's discussion on "lost relatives" in the village of Sarpi on the Turkish-Georgian border in Pelkmans, *Defending the Border*, 19–20.

issues of identity, where one's former home is no longer available to them. In other words, their homes had been replaced by impersonal and depersonalized space owing to the complete disruption of relationships and the tense atmosphere. In what remains, I want to draw upon my fieldwork experience to show how religious beliefs and practices are brought to bear upon these dynamics and later, reflect on how these actions signal underlying theological realities.

RELIGIOUS PRACTICE WITHIN CONTESTED SPACES

Daphne Berdahl, in her study of a post-Soviet divided Germany argues that borderlands are paradoxical in nature because they are zones of ambiguity yet places of intense and articulated lucidity.[30] Applying this distinction to the Gali border region reveals that what is in focus here is the dual role that the border plays in the IDP imagination as well as the social interaction that stems from that imagination. As detailed above, constructed and contested borders create ambiguity both in terms of who one is, but also in terms of where one can say he or she is from. On the other hand and perhaps more importantly for the Georgian IDP, borders also foster a certain kind of lucidity, or what I would call social memory, by reminding IDPs and reinforcing to them what was lost in war: these include both physical things like homes and graves, but also imaginaries such as a bounded and sacred historical homeland, the symbolism of historical unity, common ground, and cordial relationships. In addition, borders also reinforce a desire to recover and reclaim these lost places and memories. The implication is that borders represent both something that has been lost, as well as the possibility of creating something new.

As a navigational tool, I want to utilize Berdahl's ambiguity and clarity paradox with regard to matters of faith, religious practice, and history. What is crucial here is the ability of the border to reinforce to IDPs what was lost on the one hand, and on the other what can be reconceptualized through negotiation. This constant reminder, (both in national discourse, religious discourse, and in IDP testimonies) creates ambiguity, frustration, depression, i.e. "anxiety" in Kabachnik's terminology[31], but also the conditions for a renewed or revitalized identity. The following case study

30. Berdahl, *Where the World Ended*, 233, 141.

31. Peter Kabachnik's research in the realm of political science and geography has pointed out the role of nationalist discourse in the formation of what he calls "cartographic anxiety" regarding the territorial integrity of Georgia. See Kabachnik, "Shaping Abkhazia," 397–415; Kabachnik, "Wounds That Won't Heal," 45–60.

then addresses the way religious faith and identity seek a new clarity, or seeks to recover an old clarity, in the way it is brought to bear on the dynamics of border life described above.

The Cross-Border Mission of Father Archil

One of the most salient examples of a Georgian IDP who negotiates the realities of the contested space of the Gali region is Father Archil, a Georgian Orthodox priest. Father Archil's story is unique because he has been commissioned by the ruling Patriarch of the Georgian Orthodox Church to minister covertly within and across the border zone into Abkhazia. I first met Father Archil in his cell (Georgian *kelia*) which is the official housing complex of the priests at Tbilisi's main Trinity (Georgian *Sameba*) Cathedral. When we arrived, Father Archil greeted me and my translator with open arms and a warm invitation. Entering his room was like experiencing an ancient Orthodox service complete with all the visual accoutrements needed for a transcendent encounter. The entire space from floor to ceiling was decorated with icons encased in ornate wooden frames hand carved and painted with skill and devotion by Archil himself. Even his bed was hand hewn and beatified with carved decorative crosses and designs. In the center of the main wall of his room was a large wooden case that displayed larger and more important icons. Across the room were shelves of books, manuals, and manuscripts; the sources and inspiration of liturgies and sermons that Archil would prepare.

Spiritual Conditions of Gali: Ruined Churches and Lives

The covert nature of Father Archil's mission demanded certain explanation and legitimation. He had obtained special clearance by his Orthodox superiors to engage in this cross-border mission and he was one of only a handful of Georgian priests who were doing this. As an IDP himself and from the Gali region no less, he had sufficient knowledge of the local spiritual conditions of the people, their challenges of living near the border, and a well-articulated strategy for religious and spiritual renewal.

Abkhazia was a place that produced great wealth due in large part to agriculture and tourism. Large citrus harvests were exported to the entire Soviet Union before its breakup and Abkhazia was a tourist destination for both Moscow elites and other Black Sea countries. The material wealth, according to Father Archil, led to a growing materialism, spiritual apathy, and ultimately a lack of spiritual vision for rebuilding churches closed down during the Soviet period and those destroyed during the war with Georgia. Before Archil had become a priest he remembered regrettably that "even my own wedding party had one-thousand guests and we spent lots of money in not the right way."[32] While he had come to see the error of his misdirected wealth and had since joined the priesthood, he claimed that both Georgian's and Abkhazians "could have built the ruins but did nothing at that time."[33] Instead, according to him, their extravagant lifestyles led them to forget their history as an Orthodox people.

The ruined churches and monasteries of the Gali region and Abkhazia were symbolic of the overall spiritual condition of the people there. He expressed dismay at the numbers of people disinterested in God. Speaking of the youth he said, "Unfortunately the young people have changed in a bad way if someone talks to them about morality, they don't agree and don't want to listen to anything."[34] Furthermore, the spiritual erosion was fertile ground for other non-Christian groups to enter and begin their work. He said, "In Abkhazia, many people have turned from the truth and have turned to different sects and are doing many superstitious things . . . different groups have appeared including the Islamic fundamentalist group Wahabbism."[35]

When I asked Archil what he thought the greatest challenge for Christians in Gali was he responded that many people in the border regions do not have adequate access to priests and as a result, they could not have proper confession of their sins. When I asked him how ordinary people coped with this situation, he smiled and said, "They use mobile phones instead, but it is not the same as a real person, and besides, there is still a fear that cell phones are bugged by the authorities."[36]

STRATEGIES OF RECONCILING SPACE

I had assumed when I went to interview Archil that he was ministering to Georgians in an effort to rebuild the Georgian church. However, I found instead that he and other Abkhazians were working together to address the needs there. He said, "There are big populations of Abkhazians who

---

32. Father Archil, interviewed by the author, September 23, 2013.
33. Ibid.
34. Ibid.
35. Ibid.
36. Ibid.

live in Gali and I am ready to serve for both Abkhazians and Georgians." In fact he and other priests and laymen in the region had "renovated three churches in Abkhazia and in one church serves an Abkhazian pastor." He had clearly taken on a reconciliatory tone saying "there is no difference between IDPs or non IDPs . . . it's all the same for me."[37] Therefore, one of the strategies of his mission was to be available to both Abkhazians and Georgians, demonstrating Christian unity and reconciliation and at the same time walking a very fine line between contested visions of nationalism which the border represented.

Besides the physical danger, the challenges to Archil's ministry were numerous: first, the Georgian Orthodox church who sanctioned his ministry across the border is looked on with suspicion by the Abkhaz authorities because they view it as creeping Georgian nationalism. One of the reasons Father Archil was denied official permission to minister within Abkhazia is the perception that Georgian priests are there to sow nationalistic seeds. Secondly, Archil is an IDP himself and thus has investment on a personal level as one who has lost his home.

Despite the potential politicization of his work and the risk to his own life, Archil's strategy with regard to the Gali region was aimed at the reconciliation of Abkhazian and Georgian relations through the restoration of a lost vision of a Christian past and a lost vision of a unified homeland. This reconciliation project would be a direct confrontation to competing nationalisms, mistaken historical perceptions, and the chaos of border life. The following strategies are Archil's creative and ambiguous attempts to reconcile the chaotic space of the border.

Seeing Things Differently

The first of these strategies is discussed below as Father Archil recounts a trip into Abkhazia in the recent past. After the ceasefire agreement, the United Nations had established a monitoring office in the town of Gali (the main city of Gali region). He describes his interaction with UN officials, a somewhat neutral party to the conflict.[38]

> The Gali head office (of the UN) was on the same street where I used to live. In front of the UN office was a museum, which was completely robbed, and so the UN converted it to a storage

37. Ibid.

38. The Gali region is inside Abkhazia and functions as a buffer between Georgia and Abkhazia proper.

> unit. I tried to get in and see what was left. There were ruins of old churches with old Georgian writings. Those who robbed it fortunately did not take the stones with them. So I approached the UN office and asked if I could take the stones with me. The translator told me that I should ask the Abkhazian authorities, But I thought, 'they don't know that they're still here and I had no right to ask them.'[39]

After some negotiation with the UN staff, (who seemed slightly uninterested according to him) they arranged for a truck to come and take the stones away,

> The UN sent two trucks and helped me load the stones and now I am keeping them in my mother's house. These are the ruins of the church in the Gali region of Abkhazia. The ruins would identify who built the churches and monasteries. Of course I won't have a chance to rebuild the churches from these stones, but as the Patriarch has already indicated, at some point Abkhazians will realize that they should be together with Georgians and many have already realized this. My aim is for everyone to see these ruins. It is not a military secret to keep away from people, it is a part of our (shared) history.[40]

According to Father Archil, the ideal of a shared history is invoked through finding and publically displaying religious artifacts in Abkhazian territory. The stones in this case operate on several different levels in the popular and cultural imagination to accomplish the goal of unity. First, they operate on a *ritual* level. His aim for "everyone to see these ruins" is a call for them to see things differently as they engage in an act of religious pilgrimage. Archil says, "They have put them (the stones) in the yard in a monastery and it will be nicely kept with flowers around . . . and people will come." Secondly, the stones operate within a particular storyline of historical *memory*. For Archil, the story of the Georgian nation is a story of religious and cultural survival against larger empires and ideologies— the Ottoman Empire (Islamic rule) and in most recent memory—Communist atheism from Russia. Archil says, "These ruins are from the 7th to 11th centuries, and most of these churches were destroyed during the communist period."[41] By invoking the distant (7th to 11th cent) Islamic rule, and the more recent memory of Communist atheism, Archil also

---

39. Father Archil, interviewed by author, September 23, 2013.
40. Ibid.
41. Ibid.

subtly interrogates the role of Russia in Abkhazia's past and future. In effect he is saying that we (both Abkhazia and Georgia) survived atheistic communism under Russian rule as a result of our Orthodox faith and our future should be together as well.[42] The statement, "at some point Abkhazians will realize that they should be together with Georgians," was a common phrase repeated among other IDPs as well. Its meaning appears to be that Russia's intervention in Abkhazia and their economic and political affiliation with them will only lead them down the repeating paths of history. Finally, the stones operate in a *reconciling* fashion. They call Abkhazians to an open and mutual friendship with Georgia, one characterized by peaceful relations and a reconciled past. By contrasting a new openness available to everyone with a "military secret" he denounces the role of violence and conflict as the way in which to carve out a new future.

"When the Icon Returns to Ilory"

The second strategy that Archil uses in confronting the chaotic border space is also visual. In addition to a renewal of historical memory, Archil wanted to utilize a common religious artifact (the icon) to bring about a different way to viewing the border space. As I discussed in chapter 2, Ilory Church, built in the 11th century is one of the most famous Orthodox churches in western Georgia. Located in Ochamchire in Abkhazia, Ilory is a very meaningful site for religious and cultural identity for most of the IDPs I interviewed. Father Archil had been baptized in the church and another IDP, Tangizi Tungia, had also been baptized there. The founding of the church is connected with a hunting expedition of St. George who is the patron saint of Georgia.[43]

St. George of Ilory is also a venerated icon known for its miracles of protection and curing illnesses. One IDP, Irakli, said the following:

> It [Ilory] was the only church during the communist time functioning in Abkazia. Our population has a different approach to this place. There are a lot of legends and sayings. Some say when the icon will be back to Ilory there will be peace in Abkhazia. I cannot say the exact history, but I know that this icon can cure

---

42. For a good overview of the Georgian Orthodox church history especially focusing on the communist era, see Abashidze et al., *Witness through Troubled Times*.

43. For more information on this church, see Pipia, "Treasures of Georgia," para. 3.

people. When we don't have children, it is believed that it can cure barrenness.⁴⁴

In fact, as I visited many of the homes of IDPs during my fieldwork, there was a St. George of Ilory icon sticker on many of the doors to their houses. The icon of Saint George of Ilory is significant for other reasons besides its curing potential. Embedded within the understanding of icons in Eastern Orthodoxy is a deep and enduring connection between the founding of churches, the icons that emerge from that process and the geographical place where the church is located. In the introduction to Archpriest Zakaria Machitadze's book *Lives of the Georgian Saints* he connects biography to icon to place, thereby establishing in religious frame the connection between the biography of saintly persons and the biography of the land. He says, "The Georgian land is soaked in the blood of its people—people who gave their lives for the peace of the Church and for their motherland."⁴⁵ The biographies of person and place overlap because each icon—visual representation of the saint—is visualized within a placial scale—he or she may represent the nation, the region, the city, the village, the monastery or church and yet each place or person can represent the other in turn. Indeed, many icons feature a hand painted landscape or structure corresponding to a place in the country simply because the saint lived near or was known to have done a miracle in that place. In sum, the icon's function is in part the visual representation of a saint or holy one, whose image both summons and sustains memory of places, territories and indeed national imaginaries.

This background material brings me to the second main strategy that Archil was engaged with in his cross-border mission into Abkhazia. Inside Archil's *kelia*, I noticed two icons sitting on the floor in large wooden cases. These cases were approximately 6–8 inches deep and were covered with a glass door, allowing icons to be protected within yet visible behind the glass. These cases were hand-carved and ready for transport across the border into the Gali region of Abkhazia. As we discussed his work, it became apparent that the other aspect of Archil's mission there in addition to the display of religious stones, was an attempt to reopen churches that were closed.

To begin, he showed me an official denial letter by the ruling council on religious affairs in Sokhumi for his request to minister within

---

44. Irakli, interviewed by author, September 17, 2013.
45. Machitadze, *Lives of the Georgian Saints*, 33.

Abkhazian territory.[46] Because of this denial, he was under constant surveillance and threat by Russian peacekeepers who viewed him as a subversive threat to Abkhazian territorial integrity. Despite personal risk to himself and his helpers, Father Archil was engaged in a manufacturing campaign of icons and icon cases with which he sought to repopulate the closed down Georgian churches and reopen them. He said,

> So, sometimes we do church services in the night because of the situation, we have to be hidden. Once the icons will be done, I will deliver the icons to Zugdidi[47] and there are some guys there who will help me cross the border. There is a gap of like fifteen minutes when Russian snipers are not aiming their guns at the borderline. Guys from the Gali side are calling from their phones and saying stop, go, stop go, etc. So once the icons will be done, it will be presented to the churches. I will leave a letter from the patriarch at the churches that are sealed (closed) saying that it is the twenty-first century and it's a very big shame to lock and seal the church. So I will unlock these churches.[48]

The challenges and risks to this mission are obvious. Unlocking the churches closed down by Abkhazian authorities involves acts of religious subversion grounded in personal faith, culture, and history. 'When the icon returns to Ilory' becomes not simply a passive call to wait, but a risky faith endeavor born of historical and spiritual clarity; a sign of peace that was to come.

Father Archil's strategy was symbolic in two interrelated ways. First, the icon of Saint George had national and spiritual identities attached to it. Indeed the St. George of Ilory icon was merely a representative of the whole. For Archil, any icon crafted in Georgia and depicting Georgian saints had the 'authority' and 'presence' to reopen churches in a contested region and was a sign of religious territoriality and God's blessing.

Secondly, Archil's strategy as an IDP signaled something more complex for his own religious identity as it relates to place, personhood, and displacement. In order to understand how Archil's mission of crafting and smuggling icons is related to his own identity in displacement I would like to invoke the research of Gabriel Hanganu, who seeks to establish

---

46. For a good overview of the uneasy history between the Abkhazian and Georgian churches, see Matsuzato, "Inter-Orthodox Relations," 245–46.

47. Zugdidi is a border town on the Georgian side of the Adminisrative Border Line (ABL).

48. Father Archil, interviewed by author, September 23, 2013.

a new model for the study of Eastern Christians and communities—a model that I believe helps clarify the dimensions of Archil's actions. In his chapter "Eastern Christians and Religious Objects," Hanganu argues that social and religious lives of Eastern Christians must be understood by combining both anthropological theory and Orthodox theological anthropology. He says,

> In the particular case of Orthodox Christian icons, the theological assumption that the constitutive materials maintain an invisible connection with God is combined with the belief that the honor paid to the image passes on to whomever the image represents. This double determination of the icon, which reflects the double determination of the human person in Orthodoxy, suggests an alternative method that can be employed in the anthropological study of Eastern Christians—a method that is informed by Orthodox anthropology and focuses on the religious objects produced, circulated, and employed within the community.[49]

Foremost, Hanganu's interpretive framework involves an analysis of the ways in which the agency and biographies of material objects like icons are entangled together with those of the broader community and proceeds on the assumption that material objects, i.e. icons, churches, etc. "have the capability of accumulating histories . . . and that their "present meanings are partly determined by the persons with which they interacted and the events they were part of."[50] The thin line separating personhood and material culture is made even thinner given the devotional context and the "enhanced entangling potential of religious objects, with both the visible and invisible, the material and immaterial, realms of existence."[51]

Applying Hanganu's framework to Father Archil's actions across the border may take several interpretive trajectories. First, by virtue of his investment in fashioning icons, hand carving their cases, and hand delivering them amidst personal risk, Archil's project represents a biographical entangling with the religious icon itself and the place of its final resting. In this way, Archil, together with the icon he fashions, marks out national territory, redeems, and reconciles it. He embodies what Hanganu describes as the implications of an Orthodox view of persons and objects,

49. Hanganu, "Eastern Christians and Religious Objects," 49.
50. Ibid., 50.
51. Ibid.

that "objects created by people are part of their work of transforming nature."[52] Secondly, and related to the first, Archil's life work and mission of smuggling icons reveals a strategy that other IDPs had only spoken about; that is, the longing to return, rebuild, and resist the religious and relational chaos of the border space. As an IDP *and* priest, he has a double identity that is manifest through and because of his mission. This was made clear to me as he described the way that he visited his mother and his family's graves while he made trips across the border to reopen churches, "I sometimes go up to my yard, next to the door to check my house, but I may not visit my mother so she will not be nervous."[53]

And finally, Archil's mission cross-border cannot be seen as simply an individual exercise in reasserting his identity as an IDP and attempting to recover a lost sense of home. It must also be considered a social and a cosmic correspondence as well as set against the backdrop of the broader religious strategy of the Orthodox Church's missiological goal in the post-Soviet Era, which is now expressly applied to the contested region of Abkhazia. Consider the following quote from Silvia Serrano.

> This ostentation of orthodoxy cannot be understood only as the natural and spontaneous irruption of a religion, too long confined to privacy, into a hypothetic public sphere: it is mainly the result of a political will and of strategies aiming at re-defining the link between religion and national identity and at labeling the territory as a part of Orthodox Christendom. Building new churches is part of this strategy, since the motivation is not only to open new places of worship, but also to create a landscape reflecting the congruence of religion and national identity.[54]

Serrano's quote, while helpful, is only one dimension of the social and cosmic correspondence of Orthodoxy in displacement. This chapter has primarily highlighted one man's attempt to reconcile contested spaces out of his own religious faith and mission. But his personal mission must also be recognized as part of a larger ecclesial mission whose goal is closely entangled with that of the larger nation to which Archil belongs. This kind of ambiguity can be expected in a contested space like the border region which was set up to divide loyalties and carve out separate identities.

52. Ibid., 49.
53. Father Archil, interviewed by author, September 23, 2013.
54. Serrano, "De-Secularizing National Space," 38.

At the outset of this chapter I intended to analyze the ways in which religious faith and identities are brought to bear on the contested Gali region of Abkhazia. Studies continue to be done offering solutions and confidence building measures in order to "thaw" this particular contested region of the world. However, none of these studies expressly deal with the ways in which local Christians are offering their solutions for reconciling contested places. This chapter is an attempt at just that. What remains is to distill some preliminary thoughts on how Archil's response is also his attempt to theologize a renewed sense of place in displacement utilizing and expanding upon his own theological tradition. I will turn to this task in chapter six with the theology of the icon.

4

Places of Displacement
Home and the Remaking of Lived Places

IN THE PREVIOUS CHAPTER, I highlighted the religious and national dimensions of IDP identity by analyzing Father Archil's experience of the contested border zone between Georgia and Abkhazia. I discussed how his attempts to make public displays of ruined churches and to "bring the icons back to Ilory" were symbolic attempts to reconcile not only his own identity with where he was from, but more importantly to reconcile the space of the border from its depersonalizing state into one characterized by a shared unity and sacred past. In this chapter, I will continue the examination of how religious faith is brought to bear upon another primary location of displacement—the home. The goal of this discussion is to allow the responses of lived faith in displacement to aid in theological construction and reflection in the final chapter.

This present chapter will frame the discussion of home in two interrelated ways. For purposes of analysis they remain separate, but in reality, they make up the broad conception of home in displacement. The first way of framing the discussion on home is to look at home broadly as it is experienced among IDPs. What is it, how does it operate, and what do IDPs make of the loss of it in displacement? The second way of framing the discussion is to look at the relationship between home and faith and the way that faith language is brought to bear on losing home and recovering a sense of home.

Thus, the chapter will be organized in the following way. First, I will discuss the various themes that emerged in the ethnographic record as a way of entering into the discussion on home. Home's multidimensionality; both its temporal (past, present, future), spatial (physical location, concrete structures, homeland), and psychological (emotional, imaginary) dimensions will surface throughout in the testimonials of IDPs. Such themes will set the stage to enhance the religious significance of the home and the various dimensions of IDP faith stories in displacement. I will particularly focus the second part of the chapter on how faith in God and religious practices are mobilized, understood, and articulated in the loss and remaking of home in displacement.

WHAT IS HOME?

In the introduction of her essay, "Places of Experience and the Experience of Place," Katherine Platt says, "Places of experiences provision us with identity to venture forth out of this place into less certain or orderly spaces . . . Places of experience connect the past to the future, memory to expectation . . . home of course is the penultimate place of experience."[1] Interviewing IDPs about their conceptualizations of home revealed a complex and multidimensional experience of place full of emotion and rich with description. Analysis of the data in this regard led to several superordinate themes each with subthemes that expand and develop them. These primary themes are: 1) Home as the provision of psychological fulfillment 2) Home as a place of abundance; and 3) Home remade in the present.[2] The remainder of this section will tease each of these themes out in more detail as well as explore sub-themes that arise accordingly.

HOME AS THE PROVISION OF PSYCHOLOGICAL FULFILLMENT

By psychological fulfillment, I mean that conceptualizations of home took on qualities of emotional satisfaction during our discussions. Inevitably, when conversation turned to the war and the loss of their homes, there were feelings of deep loss. Three sub-themes that surfaced were home as: a place of emotional longing; a place of nostalgic landscapes; and loss of home: feelings of despair and hope.

---

1. Rouner, *The Longing for Home*, 112–27.

2. I am using a similar process of ethnographic reporting found in another study on the meaning of home among refugees. See Rosbrook and Schweitzer, "The Meaning of Home," 159–72.

A place of emotional longing

The participants in the study understood home as a place of emotional longing and satisfaction, made even more palpable given their loss. Expressed in the following memory by Irakli, "So I lived there for 19 years. So I cannot go there to my town, but when I am near my hometown, I feel like I am attached to this place and I am happy. So I cannot really explain, but I also miss this place ... I would stand in different places which ones that I loved. Of course I loved to be at home."[3]

Irakli focused his attachment to home in the language of proximity. Despite his inability to access his home, being "near" home, brought feelings of happiness and satisfaction. Others expressed emotional longing differently. One participant, speaking in Russian for the entire interview, switched to her first language of Georgian when she began to describe some of her best memories of home. Her switch to Georgian signaled to me a feeling of vulnerability and deep emotional desire for her home city.[4]

In an interview with an IDP named Tavila, her emotional longing for her home translated into a kind of advocacy—an attempt to prove the worth and value of her home to those who would forget or undermine its significance.[5] Tavila discussed the desirability of Abkhazia over against visiting and living in other countries. She told a story of one of her friends who had left Abkhazia to live in Portugal for a year. When her friend returned she described the conversation like this,

> I will tell you about a neighbor who lived one year in Portugal from the Gali region in Abkhazia ... She was married in Sokhumi. When they came back, both wife and husband knocked on our door and we had a visit together. And they were sitting around the table and there was a map of Sokhumi on the wall. So, we were talking about their time away and that lady said that she missed living in Portugal. My heart was broken ... I told her, "Portugal is not yours, Sokhumi is not yours, but yours is

---

3. Irakli, interviewed by author, September 17, 2013.
4. Eka, interviewed by author, September 21, 2013.
5. This is another indicator of a contested place where "space is constitutive of power" in this instance, the power of an idealized memory and origin versus the power of forgetfulness. In these and other cases resistance takes the form of social movements and local activism. See Low and Lawrence-Zúñiga, *The Anthropology of Space*, 19–20.

that village where you were born and where you started to walk, where you went to school for the first time."⁶

Tavila's advocacy was rooted in the dangerous proposition that other IDPs had forgotten their roots. And her emotional response captured by the phrase "my heart was broken" indicated the possibility of the betrayal of forgetfulness. For her friend to "miss" Portugal while sitting in front of a map of Sokhumi was to abandon her roots and even herself, it was to betray other IDPs who had kept their longings alive. Along these lines, according to Eli Wiesel, the greatest danger of exile is forgetfulness. He says, "forgetting marks the end of human experience, and of longing too . . . " it is in fact the "opposite of home."⁷

What is further important to consider in Tavila's quote is the remedy she prescribes for her friend's forgotten loyalty. Like many other IDPs' memories of home, she describes daily village life as a child as a signal of her ultimate emotional rooting and identity. She does not remind her friend of the greatness of Georgia or the beauty of Abkhazia in contradistinction to Portugal, she seeks to convince her that her village is her birthright. She says, "Yours is that village"; she implies ownership, identity, and personality; she is an extension of her village and her village is an image of her.

A place of nostalgic landscapes

Every interview contained elements of nostalgic remembering. Nostalgia (literally, "pained at the [non]return home")⁸ is reinforced by forced displacement. Julia Creet says, if "leaving is the only option, where one leaves becomes a nostalgic past."⁹ Of interest is the way in which nostalgia was directed toward landscapes in particular. One participant describes his memory of Abkhazia this way,

> When I was a student I used to have a place under the palms where I would spend one hour per day and watch the sea. If someone was there, I would wait until they left and then I would go. Sometimes I would sleep near the sea, on the beach in the

---

6. Tavila, interviewed by author, September 30, 2013.
7. Rouner, *The Longing for Home*, 24–25.
8. Casey, *Getting Back into Place*, 38.
9. See Introduction in Creet and Kitzmann, *Memory and Migration*, 10.

night, but I have not done that here (Tbilisi). There is no sea here. It's like a saved dream.[10]

This participant expressed his past life in Sokhumi as a "saved dream," a fixed nostalgic memory where not only is there a pining for past times, but a longing for past places. This kind of nostalgia for landscape is one of the clearest indicators of the power of physical location to define personal identity. As Belden Lane says, "Personal identity is fixed for us by the feel of our own bodies, the naming of the places we occupy, and the environmental objects that beset our landscape."[11]

Loss of home: feelings of despair

Lane goes on to say that if one is deprived of a "sufficient sense of placement … then we proceed to make up places with the power of our imagination."[12] If this is true for the displaced in general, then it is more so for those who have experienced forced displacement and loss.

The loss of home for many Georgian IDPs led to articulating loss in terms of despair. Eka, an IDP from Sokhumi expressed her loss in this way, "it was the great pain of my life to lose my city (of Sokhumi). Sometimes in my dreams I see the streets of Sokhumi and my house. I see a tree in my yard. It is a part of me, who I am."[13] Another IDP expressed her despair in terms of her loss of hope at the ability to ever return. While all of her memories of Sokhumi were positive, it was the protracted nature of her loss combined with the failure of any real political solutions for return that led her to say,

> [Y]ou know, I hear the country and government keep talking about it (a return) but after 20 years it gets harder and harder to believe in that. I don't think we'll go back really. To be honest, watching the TV, the seaside, the ocean of Sokhumi, I can't hold back the tears and my heart is beating very fast. When I hear the song about Sokhumi, right away I start weeping and the kids come and say "don't cry grandma, don't cry."[14]

---

10. Irakli, interviewed by author, September 17, 2013.
11. Lane, *Landscapes Of The Sacred*, 7.
12. Ibid.
13. Eka, interviewed by author, September 21, 2013.
14. Iamze, interviewed by author, September 24, 2013.

For many of the participants in the study, intense despair led to other feelings, especially blame. Blame was directed toward the governments in Tbilisi and Sokhumi, and anger toward those who had caused the war. Those participants who had actually lost family members in the war despaired at their lot in life. One woman kept asking "why did this happen to a mother of eight children?" Her despair was connected to a feeling of the intense burden of caring for her eight children after the loss of her husband.[15]

HOME AS A PLACE OF ABUNDANCE

Home as a place of abundance comprised three sub-themes: a place of material abundance; a place of relational authenticity; and loss of home: between a tourist and a resident.

Home as a Place of Material Abundance

All of the participants described Abkhazia as a desirable place because of its rich natural resources and wealth. As a region, Abkhazia was known for its seaside parks and ports, mountainous terrains and temperate climate. The local economy was more robust than Georgia due to its citrus and tea plantations, and its strategic location on the Black Sea connected Abkhazia to the wider world. In the Soviet Era, the capital Sokhumi was the primary vacation destination for Russians who needed respite from the harsh life of Russia's metropolises. My informants' testimonies all revealed a sense of desirability both for themselves and for others. One IDP describes Abkhazia this way:

> Abkhazia was more developed than the rest of Georgia ... mostly because of the sea, relationship with foreigners and being very close to Russia. I lived in Gali. There was a sports base (complex) where many foreigners would come and visit and we would interact with them. There were Germans, Czechs, and Polish. In Sokhumi, there were Italian ships coming for business along with other countries in the Soviet Union.[16]

Abundance can also be measured in terms like self-determination, ownership, and a balance of work and leisure. Participants repeated the

---

15. Tsisiana, interviewed by author, September 20, 2013.
16. Irakli, interviewed by author, September 17, 2013.

phrase "we had everything" when asked to describe life in Abkhazia. Some like Iamze went further in their explanation.

> We had such a large house, a yard, a spacious yard, like 14 rooms with a heating system, we lived really well. I grew up there. I can't tell you the favorite memory, all of our lives we knew we had to work hard . . . and we had a feeling we had to work and in the evening we would get together as a family with friends and go to the sea and beach. So we had pets, both domesticated and non- domesticated, we had jobs, everything.[17]

Home as a place of relational authenticity

All participants in the study remembered the relational elements of living in Abkhazia, although not all of them described it in detail. Neighborliness and relational warmth stood out among participants and continued to be a feature of post-war life and memory. One participant described the value of relational commitments with this example,

> Abkhazia was much better place [than Georgia]. Even the earth was better, and nature and relationships between people were very good. They were very close and friendly, they loved each other, had respect to each other. In joy or grief they helped each other. They didn't betray each other. Of course there were some negative sides, but mostly I didn't see such style of life anywhere. We can bring an example . . . I had neighbors who lived in one block of flats. Now they live in Moscow and these guys, they are not brothers, just neighbors and friends from Abkhazia. They were sending money to my parents. When he comes from time to time to visit he could even give our children presents. When we were studying in Moscow they hosted us, invited us, did everything for us. They even sent one thousand US dollars for my father's funeral . . . He is not a brother or relative, just a former neighbor.[18]

Another participant described her home as a place of hospitality and self-giving. She said, "People (In Abkhazia) would have huge houses and would rent rooms to guests, but we would never take any money for rent. We always had guests coming and they would live in our house in

---

17. Iamze, interviewed by author, September 24, 2013.
18. Tangizi Tungia, interviewed by author, October 9, 2013.

Ochamchire. It doesn't matter if we had enough food or not, if there be a piece of bread and cheese it's enough."[19]

Some participants described relational elements as they recounted their journeys out of Abkhazia in the early days of fighting. These memories all indicated a high value given to social networks, feelings of warmth toward others, and practices of hospitality with a self-giving undercurrent. For example, Tavila (A Georgian IDP) recounted this narrative about an Abkhazian man:

> So the husband of my sister left their village very soon afterwards because the Abkhazians started to attack that village very soon and they moved to Ochamchire. So my sister's family moved to a house of the sister's husband's friend ... who was a bus driver and an Abkhazian. My sister's husband knew this Abkhazian man very well. He allowed the sister's family to move into his house and he said, "If you win the war, I will leave this house and everything in it to you." But everything finished so that both Georgians and Abkhazians had to leave their houses.[20]

Also interesting to note is that the participants who described the relational warmth of being at home in Abkhazia (in the past) also related the ongoing value and 'practice' of experiencing home through relationships in their displacement. Home was experienced as connectedness to immediate family and extended networks of other IDPs. Tavila for example experienced home every time she and other IDPs would get together and share memories:

> When the family comes together, [we discuss] all our memories there ... Even the neighbors (other IDPs) when we come together we remember the time when we lived in Ochamchire ... immediately as soon as we meet together, we start to talk about that time when we lived there. Even through the Internet, when we talk to former neighbors from Ochamchire ... whether in America, Portugal, Moscow, the main subject of our conversation is Ochamchire. Of course we spent our entire childhood there and remember that time ...[21]

---

19. Tavila, interviewed by author, September 30, 2013.
20. Ibid.
21. Ibid.

Loss of Home: Between a Resident and Tourist

Experiencing the loss of home again and again seemed to play out not only in shared memories, but also in the tangible process of property ownership and management. One participant, Irakli, was both an IDP and the Director of Social Programs Foundation, a non-governmental organization providing information, counseling, and legal assistance to IDPs in Georgia. Irakli described the greatest current challenge for IDPs as home ownership. In the course of the interview, it was apparent that this present challenge continually reinforced the desire to have access to their houses in Abkhazia. This confirms a study done by Peter Kabachnik suggesting that current IDP housing concerns continually remind them of what they lost.[22]

Every participant in the study owned a home with land and desired to see it and manage it. In addition, each participant was aware that their homes were no longer the same as they left them, but regardless, they felt they should have the right to manage their property. Irakli said, "I want to enjoy right of ownership and manage my property. It's not up to me whether I can live there or not live there, but it's my property, so why should I not manage it?"[23]

Managing property in a contested zone no longer governed by the Georgian government is risky at best and impossible at worst. All of the participants in my study with the exception of one had not visited their former homes in Sokhumi personally. One person had managed to go back four times in the first two years after the war at great personal risk. Others, not participants in my study, living near the border region have had greater chances to return, yet their proximity to the border does not guarantee easy passage. Many participants' homes are either no longer standing or are in serious disrepair. Some were destroyed by war, others by weather. One participant told me that on her property stood Russian military equipment and even the equipment was overgrown with weeds. One of my participant's family members traveled to Ochamchire to see her home and reported this, "My niece said lately that they tried to find their house in Ochamchire. They could not. There are no houses anymore because the forest has grown over it. So if they will allow our people, to

---

22. Kabachnik et al., "Where and When Is Home?," 323.
23. Irakli, interviewed by author, September 17, 2013.

go back ... there are no houses there, only the forest and trees ... But in a couple of years, everything will be the same as it was before."[24]

In all of these testimonies, memory had staged a confrontation between a nostalgic past and the present and future reality of home-loss. To visit without permanently returning was to be reminded of everything that was lost, and yet in the perceptions of many, merely visiting meant taking on the identity of a tourist:

> When I was coming back to Tbilisi my mother was stopping me ... and I was looking at the beautiful sea and around this beautiful nature and everything around me seemed to be dead. It was as if the trees were crying. If we will be able to go back, I would not like to go back and see this dead town, I want to remember this town as it was, as a beautiful place. I don't want to go back to visit, I would go back and rebuild.[25]

The resulting state among many IDPs was the seemingly impossible position of being between a resident and a tourist in relation to their former homes. However, as the next section will elaborate, there are some IDPs who have managed to remake their lives and homes in spite of the tension they feel.

REMAKING HOME IN DISPLACEMENT: ESTABLISHING CONTINUITY WITH THE PAST

The process of remaking home in the context of prolonged and multiple displacements is by no means a uniform or homogenous enterprise in the IDP experience. First, there is no uniform IDP experience of displacement. Their journeys out of Abkhazia were different. Some had time to plan and leave, others fled in the night on foot and others were taken by bus or car. Some IDP homes were left intact; other homes were destroyed completely. Some mothers saw their husbands and children killed. Some children saw their fathers and mothers killed. Some had neighbors in Abkhazia who helped them escape and others' neighbors became a source of betrayal and fear.

Their arrival into other parts of Georgia or Russia was also different. Some were welcomed into the homes of extended family members; others slept in dilapidated buildings. Some fled to Russia and experienced other types of estrangements while others moved in with complete strangers

24. Tavila, interviewed by author, September 30, 2013.
25. Ibid.

near the ceasefire line waiting until they could return. As one woman said, "We moved through Enguri (administrative border), through Dixazurga.[26] I remember that the whole village gathered together and all left together, in my cousin's large vehicle. No one took anything with them, just documents. For some reason everybody thought that we would be back soon. People did not understand that it was war . . . "[27]

In the current situation, political, economic, and cultural factors also play a role in how home is remade in displacement. As discussed previously, governmental policies toward IDPs have had a significant role in resettlement efforts throughout Georgia. During my fieldwork, I was scheduled to interview an IDP family that was a contact I had received from a friend. The morning I called to confirm the time, he informed me that he no longer knew where the family lived because the previous day the government had opened remodeled flats and given them keys to their new home. NGO's have also played a role in helping IDPs resettle and reintegrate. On one of my trips to a refugee camp called Tserovani, I noticed that each IDP family was given a small private house with a yard where they could plant a garden and raise small livestock. The NGOs understood the importance for IDPs of having a plot of ground to cultivate as a priority in economic viability and resettlement. Larger resettlement strategies however tend to obfuscate smaller more intimate details of stories of remaking home. These stories highlight emotional and spiritual resources by IDPs themselves and demonstrate how faith is brought to bear upon finding a sense of home again.

In the remainder of this section, I want to observe and describe the ways in which some IDPs are remaking a sense of home in the present. By way of introduction, I would like to set the stage for the home making practices by pointing out several examples of IDP attempts to remake their current dwelling places with artifacts or spatial similarities brought from their former homes. I will then show how this same pattern of 'bringing forward' the past into the present describes the way in which faith operates as well in remaking home. Finally I will conclude with some preliminary thoughts about how the future is understood from a faith perspective from the IDP experience.

Rebuilding the present expressed itself in different ways in the IDP experience. The most common was to tell a story of a significant linkage

---

26. A village in the Gali District
27. Teah testimony, in Losi and Tavartkiladze, *A Heavy Burden*, 28.

with the past that was brought forward in their present living situation. David Pekaliani for example told me that a close friend was able to sneak into Sokhumi to his old home (which was by that time destroyed by weather) and gather a special fruit that was still growing in their old garden. This fruit was of special significance for David because according to him, his home and garden was the only place where this fruit grew on their street in Sokhumi. The fruit was important because it was not only symbolic of his yard and garden, it also grew and thrived in the soil where his house was during and after the war. After receiving a bushel of this famed fruit, David celebrated the New Year with all of his family and friends by making a special drink and sharing it. Then he took the remaining shoots from the plant and replanted the fruit in his mother's garden as a reminder of their home in Abkhazia.

Another IDP, Irakli, told how he and his brother managed to take a piece of an old wooden trough from their home in the Gali region with which they stomped grapes during harvest to make wine. He and his brother built a new house in Georgian controlled territory and used the wood from the trough to construct part of the wall. This served as a permanent reminder of life and home before displacement.

Still another IDP, Iamze, showed me her yard and garden that she cultivated in displacement. She described that the layout, the plants, and the table and chairs all were situated in a spatially intentional way corresponding to her garden in Sokhumi. In this way, the past was relived each day in the various artifacts that were made to decorate, cultivate or imagine the present.

Remaking home as the above stories indicate hinges largely upon the idea of establishing continuity with the past. To the extent that past artifacts, memories, patterns, decorations, etc. can be recovered, displayed or memorialized in some way, the home is on its way toward being remade in displacement.

FAITH NARRATIVES IN DISPLACEMENT

In the following section I will seek to observe and describe the way that faith is utilized in remaking a sense of home in displacement. First of all, it will be important to understand how religious narratives and their interpretations form the backstory of their loss of home. In other words, what are the raw materials used, both in memory and experience, that give IDPs a sense of a blueprint for what their present and future homes might look like? Only after this step is it possible to understand how these materials are placed in new environments to provide continuity between the home that was lost and their present homes.

Being Led—Away from home

When the Georgian-Abkhazian conflict came close enough to require a decision to stay or leave, many Orthodox believers like Eka left unprepared for the journey that was ahead. Eka, unmarried at the time of the war, left Sokhumi on Sept 27th 1992 with her three sisters, her father, and her two nephews. She had heard that if they could get to a town called Chuberi, at the Eastern end of lower Svaneti—a mountainous district of Georgian controlled territory adjacent to Abkazia—there would be busses that would take refugees to the surrounding areas and possibly to Tbilisi.

The road to Chuberi was hard. She recalled that the second biggest decision she made after deciding to leave was which path to take away from Sokhumi. According to her, most families decided to take the main road out of the city, but their family decided that it would be safer to take a narrow path through the woods into the mountains. Many families escaping at that time traveled at night and hid during the day. She told me that she never knew what happened to the people who took the main road out.

Once they were far away from the fighting and the looting, they walked in the mountains (above the tree line). She reminded me that it was late September when winter was beginning to set in the mountains of lower Svaneti and very cold. As they walked, she remembered a line of people as far as she could see in front of her going up over mountains and disappearing down into valleys. She heard the cries of little children as she walked and she could not tell how many people were in front or behind. After nine days of walking they arrived in Chuberi on October 6th, 1992.

Eka told me that as they walked, she would say the Lord's Prayer, and other simple prayers—any other thing that came to mind. She believed that "God led them out" and "showed them the way," since she nor her family had never been to Chuberi. She told a story of God leading them and how two young girls became separated from the group as they traveled and were feared dead. Since they had come very near bogs they assumed that perhaps the girls stepped into the bogs and had died.

Sometime later, the girls just "appeared out of nowhere" and told them that a man found them. He was dressed in a long priest's gown with a black hood. He told the girls to follow him quickly, and was careful not to reveal his face to them. When the larger group was within view, he told them to go and rejoin them. When they turned around to thank him, he was gone. The girls said that they did not remember what language he spoke or how long they walked, but only that someone was there to guide them back to the group.

Eka's recounting of these events as they happened nearly twenty years earlier represented the way God was continuing to lead, guide and protect them. Her interpretation of the black robed man was that "it must have been an angel and the guiding hand of God" that had saved those two girls and demonstrated his guidance and protection of their group. As she concluded her story she spoke of her current experience of God's guidance in terms of closeness and providential care. She said, "I always feel close to God" and "nothing happens without God . . . even you coming here was of God."[28]

As the above story demonstrated, the experience of divine intervention in terms of guidance and protection was brought forward from the past and acted as a way of experiencing God throughout the journey of displacement. Being led away from home was merely the beginning of being led elsewhere and into a new home. Divine guidance and protection had become for Eka a rehearsal of what Andrew Lester calls a "functional future story." Functional future stories are "future projections of our core narratives that open up life and invite us into an exciting and meaningful tomorrow."[29] Her experience of God on the journey out of Abkhazia became a story that structured her experience; and though born in the past, her ongoing faith allowed her to see her life under God's guiding hand.

Home as the Re-Creation of Sacred Spaces

Tavila is an IDP who was described to me by others as a very special woman and very sincere in her Orthodox faith. Since I was studying religious identity among IDPs I knew that it was important for me to sit and talk with her about her experience of displacement. When we arrived, we walked up four flights of stairs and entered into a large hallway that was under construction. As we entered Tavila's flat, immediately in front

---

28. Eka, interviewed by author, September 21, 2013.
29. Lester, *Hope in Pastoral Care*, 125.

of me was a large section of her living room wall and corner with many different icons displayed. I counted forty-eight icons, some were small and others larger and there was a small table, underneath which sat an incense holder, a small candle stand and several other icons with stands.[30] The assemblage, maintenance, and practices associated with the icon corner was learned by Tavila from an early age. She like other IDPs interviewed, "took the faith like a child takes its mother's milk" growing up in a religious setting where faith was not only discussed in the home, but made visual through practice.

The Icon Corner—"The Sanctuary of the Home"

In a study on homes and icons in Russia, Kira Tsekhanskaia says, "Icons occupied a special place in home rituals: newborns were touched to them, people were blessed with an icon before a wedding, a journey, or becoming soldiers … before the household icons they held prayer services on feast days and at times of misfortune, they found comfort in their grief."[31] In Nielsen's study on icons in the Georgian home he says, that it was a "sanctuary of the home" or a "little church" meant to "expand and distribute the distinctive sphere of holiness characteristic of the church building, channeling that special power into the Georgian Orthodox home."[32]

According to Tavila, she maintained this icon corner (also called beautiful corner) not because it was beautiful, but because "we have no way out from God"—seeming to suggest that she was never away from the presence and gaze of God. The question to be raised here is what is the role of the icon corner in displacement, especially when notions of 'home' and a sense of home is somewhere between the imagination of the past and the present? And furthermore, does displacement alter the way the icon corner is approached or conceived?

---

30. See Figure 5 on page 109.
31. Tsekhanskaia, "The Icon in the Home," 20.
32. Nielson, "Icons and Agency," 222.

78   Theologizing Place in Displacement

Figure 5: Tavila and her Icon Corner in Tbilisi

Tavila's answer to these questions comes in the form of a story she told about her icon corner in her house in Ochamchire:

> After the war started, I visited my house 4 times . . . during these 13 months. So this is the period during the war, not after Sokhumi was lost. The last visit was close to the time when we lost Abkhazia. It was June and I could see my house [the windows

were broken and the sofas were broken] and I started to scream. And then I heard the sound of guns. In the house [opposite of our house] was an old lady and there was one person not far in another house. When I started to scream, they started to shoot the guns and the old lady when she came out she said, "they are shooting from a close distance, so go somewhere!" And I cannot remember many things, but I went back and decided to take a video of the house. I saw a man who I knew and we worked together and he came toward me and greeted me and asked, "What happened to you?" I could not answer and stopped the taxi. I sat down and he did the same [in the taxi]. But I could not say anything to the taxi driver . . . I said, just go. So I found a person who could take the video and brought him with me and my brother in Zugdidi heard that I went to Abkhazia and he came for me from Zugdidi to Ochamchire . . . and he asked "What are [you] doing? Why are you doing this?!" When I brought the guy with the video and when we went into the house I had a corner in the room with icons and in the kitchen I had a big picture of my brother with a knife in it. He was fighting in the war. In the corner where my icons were, nothing was touched there . . . maybe they were scared to see so many icons, I don't know . . . other things were cut by a knife—furniture, blankets, clothes, etc. were torn. We took this video and my brother hid it in his clothes and we left.[33]

Tavila's interpretation of this event had several different facets: 1) it demonstrated that sacred spaces like icon corners were sources of respect even during wartime and helped her think more positively about those who destroyed her home. She pointed out that whoever did this were certainly not Chechen Muslims for example (who operated as mercenaries at the time of the war) but had some kind of Christian conscience. 2) The story also functioned to situate her home within the context of sacred space, strengthening the link between the two and as Katherine Platt said, provisioned her "with identity to venture forth out of this [Abkhazian home] place into less certain or orderly [displaced] spaces."[34] 3) Finally, this event convinced her of the importance of viewing the icon corner as an essential factor in making home in displacement because it provided a sense of sacred continuity between and within the chaotic space of displacement. From her house in Ochamchire to her flat in Tbilisi, the icon

---

33. Tavila, interviewed by author, September 30, 2013.
34. Rouner, *The Longing for Home*, 112–27; parenthesis mine.

corner provided religious continuity, a sacred connection with home and a reinforcement of her Orthodox identity in displacement.

Remaking Home: The Role of Family and Faith

Establishing familiar social networks, and in particular family support networks was another feature remaking home in displacement. After describing to me her long journey out of Abkhazia to Tbilisi, Eka spoke about how she started her new life in a new city. "I make my home with love . . . everything is love. When I arrived in Tbilisi from Abkhazia, my fiancé and I decided to get married and start a family after one month. It was truly a heroic act because we had nothing, no prospects for a job, no income, nothing. All we had is faith. Faith gives me the strength to carry the heaviest things."[35]

Remaking home in displacement continues to be a risky endeavor. In the early days of her arrival into Tbilisi, the Georgian government did not have a strategy to accept or integrate Eka and the large numbers of IDPs flooding in. Rather, IDPs would occupy any space they could, including large hotels or unfinished apartment blocks. Starting a family within the first month in this kind of environment—without a job or income—was a heroic act of faith which had been formed from her childhood and tested in her displacement from Abkhazia. As Eka's story above revealed, she believed that God superintended the journey through the mountains, with God's guiding hand leading and protecting them. Remaking home in Tbilisi was no different. Though they had nothing, they had faith enabling them to "carry the heaviest burden" and thereby take the greatest risks.

Another woman I interviewed was older when she was displaced from Abkhazia. She was fortunate enough to have brought the majority of her family members with her with the exception of her husband who died during the war. Her way of making home in a new place relied heavily upon the role her extended family took in her well-being. She referred to her family network as the only thing that was keeping her alive:

> So we have large family and very close connections and this really helps us and saves us. It keeps us going, we help each other. When you are drowning in the water, you have many family members to help you. If something bad happens we support

---

35. Eka, interviewed by author, September 21, 2013.

each other. You have to help yourself in some way . . . this is the life we live.³⁶

On the day of the interview, I did not realize that it was her seventy-third birthday. In typical Georgian hospitality, she invited me in and gave me some of her birthday cake and some grapes that she had just bought from the market. Eventually all of her children and one or two grandchildren arrived as well and I was able to see them and the way they loved and took care of her. In fact, one of her daughters acknowledging that her mother was getting old jokingly said to her mother, "You are not allowed to die until I tell you . . . you have to get written permission from me to give to Gabriel before you are allowed to die and go to heaven."³⁷

Livelihood strategies among Georgian IDPs have been the subject of a major study funded through the National Science Foundation at the University of Arizona. This project dubbed, "Georgia IDP Project: post conflict livelihoods and social networks" sought to analyze how IDPs "use social networks in the construction of livelihood strategies (means of accumulating resources for human security, both material and non-material, and financial and in-kind)." One of their presentations, entitled "How Dynamic is the Structure of Employment and Well-being" found that Abkhazian IDPs sought well-being—defined as access to employment or resources—through the "everyday collective economy and networks of survival."³⁸ The above story of Tsisiana substantiated the claims that this study discovered. Other interviews I conducted found similar patterns where social and family networks were highly influential in reintegration and/or settlement.

However, as I have argued in this book, the role of faith in remaking place and home among IDPs has itself been displaced from the discussion and should be taken into account as a strategy alongside the others. The following story told by a middle-aged IDP named Iamze demonstrates the intersection of faith, employment, and the interior lives of IDPs whose faith also counts for a sense of well-being.

> Once I was in Tbilisi . . . I used to work and I was about to lose my job . . . I was sitting and I had a vision. I saw a man who looked tall and had dark hair and a white beard. I felt a very positive energy. He wasn't speaking to me, but I felt that he wanted

36. Tsisiana, interviewed by author, September 20, 2013.
37. Ibid.
38. Mitchneck and Carboni, "How Dynamic," slide 4.

to bless me and give me the best. I realized that someone was protecting me for sure and I just remember saying [to myself] "that there is nothing to be afraid of no matter which way I go." Someone was protecting me. I saw the face, and once I was looking at the different pictures of the icons [at home] it looked like St. Nicolas. I knew right away . . .[39]

Remaking a sense of place and home to the Orthodox Christian IDP was in part guided and influenced by the religious belief system of Orthodoxy, and the rituals and beliefs that accompany it. In this and other instances, saints played a role in shaping perceptions of life and future through their active communication with Orthodox believers. In this way, saints and the icons representing them becomes an active and powerful extended family network that is relevant for everyday life in displacement. Why this is the case is the subject of later chapters, but for now, these ethnographic findings are crucial to help in building the theological reflection to come.

This chapter has covered the multidimensionality of home as conceptualized by Georgian Orthodox IDPs. It has also featured the religious aspects of understanding home in terms of losing and finding home again. This was seen in the way the journey away from home was given theological importance as well as how remaking home happened through ritual and through extended family (both biological and supernatural) networks and agents. The next chapter will explore further the connection between faith and displacement by looking at the topic of gravesites and their impact upon IDPs.

---

39. Iamze, interviewed by author, September 24, 2013.

5

Places of Displacement

Graveyards and Reimagining Place

I miss walking in my town, going to the cemetery. The cemetery has been abandoned for so many years. There's no one who goes to clean the graves there. I would tell Abkhazians: let's live together and well. We miss that place and those people very much.

—Nargiza, IDP[1]

THE PREVIOUS CHAPTERS ON borders and homes have focused on the places that inform Orthodox IDP faith and religious identity in displacement. This current chapter will focus on the ways Orthodox IDPs negotiate gravesite obligations to ancestors at burial grounds no longer accessible to them.

According to a recent survey conducted among Georgian IDPs from Abkhazia, visiting gravesites of ancestors was the second most cited reason for wanting to return to Abkhazia behind their desire to manage their properties.[2] In a recent news article, Molly Corso reported that IDPs feel most stress around Easter, the time of year when their Orthodox faith encourages a return to the gravesites to honor the dead and

---

1. Nargiza, quoted in http://www.internal-displacement.org/idmc/website/idpvoices.nsf/%28httpLifeStories%29/F33956B9CBDF85A3C1257408005744C9?OpenDocument (accessed March 4th, 2014).

2. Frichova, *Displacement in Georgia*, 6.

perform various rituals.³ She went on to say that many IDPs undertake dangerous journeys and risk imprisonment during the Easter season.

The issue of visiting graves is problematic on at least two fronts: first and foremost it is a problem of access. As the chapter on borders demonstrated, access to Abkhazia where gravesites are located remains fraught with both internal and external risks. Access issues pertain not only to the risk of border-crossings, but to the challenges of identifying unmarked graves, locating grave sites that have now been swallowed up by natural growth of forests, and the real possibility that relatives will never find the deceased body. Additionally, there are challenges of traumatic memories associated with the details of death. Many families were not able to perform proper burials; fire or wild animals destroyed remains and others were killed as they fled and are missing. Depending upon the circumstances of death, memories are more or less traumatic, but are normally characterized by a longing to visit the dead body's resting place wherever that may be.

Consequently, visiting graves is a problem for the performance of ongoing memorial rituals rooted in culture and Orthodox religious tradition. As demonstrated in the previous chapter on homes, ritual continuity was an important factor in remaking home in displacement. In that case, Orthodox IDPs reconstituted sacred spaces in the home through icon corners, maintaining a significant although altered spatial/symbolic link between their homes in Abkhazia and their current dwelling places. For gravesites no longer accessible, religious rituals cannot be performed as expected. The obligations to visit graves of family members and the inability to perform these rituals because of access issues according to one of my informants made him feel "frustrated and oppressed."⁴

This chapter is an attempt to understand the impact of displacement upon ritual obligations at gravesites. What happens when a devout Orthodox believer cannot go back to his ancestral gravesites and perform the necessary rituals? How does the inability to return, or in many cases, the impossibility of finding bodies that were buried in unmarked graves impact the religious identity and practice of surviving family members? How in fact does one accommodate his or her belief system (as the case may be) when one can no longer practice what is considered essential religious duty?

3. Corso, "For IDPs, Orthodox Easter," para.3.
4. Irakli, interviewed by author, September 17, 2013.

In an attempt to answer these questions, the chapter will be structured in the following way. The first section will provide some illustrations both in literature and in personal testimonies of IDPs regarding the general importance of a burial place for the deceased. The second section will lay out some general features of the Georgian Orthodox burial practices at the time of death and focus on the re-establishment of relational contact with the deceased. In the final section I will seek to understand from the ethnographic record ways in which IDPs adapt these practices within the context of displacement where access to plots are contested.

BURIAL SITES: A PLACE OF NATIONAL AND RELIGIOUS IMAGINATION

To speak of burial sites and the obligations surrounding them requires that you first grasp the commitment to a national and religious connection between the history of Christianity, the Georgian national struggle for survival and the lineage of saints and believers who have died on its soil. In this regard, Ilia II, the Catholicos-Patriarch of All Georgia has written, "when we reflect on our past, we are astonished at how the Georgian nation has retained its language, its Christian Faith, and its culture despite all the resistance it has faced. Our fortitude and spiritual endurance appear to be rooted in the unshakable Christian soil on which we stand ... we must continue the great works for which our forefathers died."[5] His statement, made in the context of a call to build churches and monasteries highlights the sacred connection between remembrance of the dead and the national imagination of Christianity's survival.

The connection between sacred national imaginary and burial sites has been well established in the literature.[6] Anthony Smith highlights the significance of soldier cemeteries for solidifying national identities in post-World War II Europe. Likewise, memorials of Holocaust victims and survivors allow for collective grief and national solidarity around traumatic histories.[7] Bouchard's study of Russian burial grounds also highlights the ways in which cemeteries collectivize grief in the national

---

5. Machitadze, *Lives of the Georgian Saints*, 34.

6. For example, see Anderson, *Imagined Communities*; Coulanges, *The Ancient City*; Davies, *Death, Ritual and Belief*; Foucault and Miskowiec, "Of Other Spaces," 22–27. Also see Peterson's "The Altar of the Dead"; Smith, *Chosen Peoples*; Bouchard, "Graveyards," 345–62; Verdery, *The Political Lives of Dead Bodies*.

7. Smith, *Chosen Peoples*, 243–53.

imagination gathering up sentiment and personal loyalties on a local, regional, and national scale.⁸

The connection between homeland, religion and cemetery is elaborated by many IDPs in personal testimonies about being forced from their homes. The following example is especially salient. Tamazi, a Georigan IDP spoke of his displacement as being cut off from his roots. He says, "I, a native Georgian, as well as many others older than me, cannot get used to the fact that we were cut off from our roots . . . I couldn't give up my roots, my [family's] graves, the churches of my ancestors." Tamazi continues, " . . . in Georgia, even if you own three flats in three different Georgian towns, you still have one place where your roots are, where you want to be buried."⁹ The power of burial grounds to define roots and loyalties across time and space is exemplified in the following example from local literature. Fazil Iskander is a famous Abkhazian writer who humorously celebrates and exaggerates Abkhazian customs in the face of the monolithic Soviet Union. He tells a story about Uncle Sandro, an Abkhaz farmer whose loyalty to burial customs leads him to creatively negotiate for the dead bodies of his relatives from Russian soldiers who had killed them. In the story, Iksander contrasts the extreme measures that Uncle Sandro takes to recover deceased relatives against the easily persuaded Russian soldiers guarding them. Though the story is not Georgian in and of itself, it nevertheless approximates the abiding loyalties to land, deceased relatives, and burial customs that likewise characterize Georgian customs. In the middle of his story Iskander provides a parenthetical pause and writes,

> According to Abkhazian custom a dead man must be committed to the earth in his family burying ground. If he died or was killed very far from home, one must bring him home at any cost. If he was killed by the authorities, and they are guarding his body, one must steal the corpse or seize it by force, even at the risk of one's life. Such is the law of the mountains, the Abkhazian's code of honor. And no matter how many years have passed since the loved one died or was slain, when an Abkhazian learns where he was buried, even if it is a thousand kilometers away, even if he has to sell all his property to do it, he must move his relative's remains. For Abkhazians believe that the bones of an Abkhazian in alien soil are waiting, they must be committed to their native

---

8. Bouchard, "Graveyards," 345–62.

9. Life Stories, Tamazi, found at http://www.internal-displacement.org/idmc/website/idpvoices.nsf/%28httpLifeStories%29/24FC53DC74F0D366C125741C003F3254?OpenDocument#anchor13 (accessed March 4th, 2014).

soil. Only there will they find rest, and release the souls of their relatives.[10]

As Iksander indicates, burial grounds are important not only for their location, but for the ways in which local or family soil allows for the departed soul to find rest.

A final illustration from my own fieldwork in the Fall of 2013 demonstrates the
continued link between native soil and souls at rest from the perspective of an IDP's last wishes at death. One of my translators named Tsisi told me a story about her two uncles Shota and Batu. Both uncles were well known in Sokumi, having been raised there from childhood. Shota was a lawyer in the community known for his honest work practice and his brother Butu was a respected doctor. After they fled the war in Abkhazia, Shota attempted a return visit to his home three times without success. During the final visit he did not return to Tbilisi. Tsisi informed me that he was last seen on the Enguri Bridge and many family members assumed that he had been killed attempting to cross. After 6 months, Batu went to look for him, to try to find his brother's dead body. There was no success. But after two months passed, Shota one day appeared in Tbilisi. He had been spotted at the bus station by an Abkhazian friend and was sent to his relatives in Tbilisi. When he arrived, his family noticed that he had been injured and had severe memory loss. He did not recognize any of his family except his brother-in-law. After two long months of sickness he died at the end of April 2002. He told his brother Batu before he died, "I tried to go back to my home in Sokhumi, but I could not. But as soon as you return to Abkhazia, come to my grave and tell me that we are back to Abkhazia now." As Tsisi told me this story, her eyes welled up with tears and said, "If we are allowed to go back to Abkhazia, I will rebury my uncle there."[11]

These illustrations establish the sacred connection between the deceased and the land further elaborated in the connection between the cemetery and the soul at rest. Herein lies the crucial factor of cemeteries that I will elaborate on in the next section: their religious and sacral importance in the mourning process and an ongoing relational connection to the dead in displacement.

10. Iskander, *Sandro of Chegem*, 117–18.
11. Tsisi, interviewed by author, September 30, 2013.

MAINTAINING RELATIONSHIP BETWEEN THE LIVING AND THE DEAD: GENERAL FEATURES OF GEORGIAN ORTHODOX VIEWS ON DEATH

In his classic work in anthropology *Celebrations of Death*, Metcalf and Huntington believe that the "issue of death throws into relief the most important cultural values by which people live their lives and evaluate their experiences."[12] In the Georgian context, and specifically for Orthodox Christians, belief about death is informed primarily by Orthodox religious tradition, scripture, and rituals; embodied, communicated, and performed by priests at funerals.

Lizette Larson-Miller describes the basic shape of Eastern Orthodox death rituals as three stations or sequences of rituals taking place in various locations over a set number of days. The first station is in the home where the deceased body is brought after death. In the home friends and relatives participate with priests in hymns, scripture readings and lamenting. The next station occurs as the family makes a procession to the church where songs, hymns, and scriptures are said over the dead body in front of the door of the church as a sign of entrance into the next life. Larson-Miller says, "The beginning of the liturgy at the door represents the liminality of the soul between heaven and earth."[13] The final station occurs at the cemetery where both priest and family recite prayers and perform mourning rituals such as throwing handfuls of dirt over the grave, making the sign of the cross, final blessings and prayers, and the priest's dismissal in peace.[14]

Larson-Miller's description is by and large an accurate representation of the structure of Orthodox funerals. Her description does not however recount the ongoing rituals, practices, and liturgies that have taken shape in Orthodox tradition and in popular practice over time. These rituals are based in an ongoing relationship with the deceased ritualized by the act mourning and the obligations of visiting graves.

Relationship Established and Maintained in Mourning Rituals

The view of the deceased person takes on a new dimension in the mourning process that both establishes and further maintains relational contact.

---

12. Metcalf and Huntington, *Celebrations of Death*, 25.
13. See Larson-Miller, "Roman Catholic," 116.
14. Ibid.

In a study on the lamenting practices at Georgian funerals, Helga Kotthoff observes two features of lamenting important for this study: the act of addressing the deceased, and the value of "communality" in the remembrance process.

The lament ritual in a Georgian funeral is called *xmit natirlebi* meaning, "crying loudly with one's voice," and is characterized by a variety of sounds, songs, and phrases. Kotthoff observes, "cries of grief and appeals to the deceased occur, they are spoken or sung in lines (pulse units), using crying sounds (mostly at the end of lines), voice changes, drawn-out sighs, slowly falling intonation contours with integrated peaks, bowed bodily postures and an expressive lexicon."[15] For example, in a dialogue between a mourning daughter (Ciala) and her deceased mother (Maria), Ciala says,

> I like your clan, mother, the Tshuguashivilis clan mother, you are a woman of a good clan, woman, you must not leave this clan, mother. There is no one in Tshuguaanis who would not come and express sympathy mother, everyone showered you with tears mother. You were a good wise woman, everyone liked you mother, Oh precious mother, I like your nice character mother mother . . . why did you leave us.[16]

Kotthoff goes on to describe that Georgian laments, "contrast in detail a desolate present with an idyllic past."[17] The past memorials include praise for the deceased person in the context of former life situations revealing a "complex management of address and intertextuality by reporting numerous dialogues in which either the deceased, other deceased friends and relatives or those present were involved."[18]

The lamenting rituals also situate the deceased in a larger and more expansive community of relatives both alive and dead. In addition to the deceased body and relatives in the room there is a small table with an arrangement of candles and pictures of previously deceased relatives prompting Kotthoff to observe that "a community of the dead is thereby already created in the arrangement of the room."[19]

---

15. Kotthoff, "Affect and Meta-Affect," 149–72.
16. Ibid., 157–58.
17. Ibid., 150.
18. Ibid.
19. Ibid., 154.

Grave Relations, Visiting and Maintaining Contact with the Dead

The mourning rituals described above establish *post-mortem* relational contact which is expanded further in the ongoing relationship of the living community of relatives and friends with the deceased through the act of visitation.[20] The relationship is based in core doctrinal beliefs about the waiting period between death and the resurrection, a period in which the body is believed to be at rest in the cemetery and the soul is undergoing preliminary judgment before the final judgment.[21] Regarding the state of the body and the value placed on the communal gathering at the cemetery, the Eastern father John Chrysostom in his homily "On the Cemetery's Name and the Cross" says,

> For what cause did our fathers, leaving their houses of prayer in the city, establish the practice of assembling outside the city on this day and in this very place? In as much as here rests a multitude of the departed, today Jesus Christ went down to the dead; thus we also gather here. Why, this very place is called a place of sleep (cemetery), that you might know that they [who] have died and lie here have not died, but rest and sleep.[22]

The cemetery in Orthodoxy takes on several layers of importance: First it is the site at which the resurrection will take place based upon Jesus visiting the dead in order to lead them out of death into life. Secondly, the cemetery is a site at which the living relatives honor the memory of the dead and are reminded of the conviction that they "have not died, but rest" and finally the cemetery has become a place of visitation where the community of relatives and friends aid in the judgment and afterlife of the deceased.[23]

In popular religious practice according to Kotthoff's observations, maintaining contact means placing food and drink on the graves of their dead at every major holiday or feast day—especially Easter. The dead

---

20. Visiting graves is a general feature of Orthodoxy around the world. For example see the dissertation by Ingram which studies the relational dynamics of the living and dead in Ukrainian culture. In Ingram, "The Dearly Not-Quite Departed."

21. It is beyond the scope of this chapter to trace the doctrinal and historical developments of Orthodox belief about death.

22. Chrysostom, "On the Cemetery's Name and the Cross."

23. On this latter point, the obligations to aid loved ones in the afterlife is a feature of folk Orthodoxy believed and practiced by the majority of the faithful.

receive forty days provision for their journey into the after-life, a traditional period at the end of which lies the judgment.²⁴ They are customarily brought a plate of food and drink on the second, seventh, and fortieth days and also on the first year anniversary. Wine is poured over the grave and the mourners carry and place a lit candle on the grave stone during these times. Later there is at least one commemorative day per year. Graves must be cleaned and maintained.²⁵

Figure 6: Well Maintained Orthodox Gravesite at Stepensminda Cemetery, Kazbegi Georgia. Sept. 2013.

The above descriptions of gravesite practices are supported by my own observations. One morning during my fieldwork I decided to observe and document some of the general features of an Orthodox cemetery in the mountain village of Stepansminda with a friend, Mamuka. After we drove through the small village we came to the graveyard on the outskirts. We parked our jeep and slowly ascended up the hill into a scattering of graves, what felt like another small village for the deceased. We

---

24. See where Bouchard's description of the fortieth day is especially significant because it is when the soul's fate is decided. In Bouchard, "Graveyards: Russian Ritual and Belief Pertaining to the Dead," 335.

25. Kotthoff, "Affect and Meta-Affect," 154, and see n23.

saw gravesites big and small, close enough that you could walk through, but wide enough for groups of friends and relatives to gather. Some had been kept very clean and tidy and some had fallen into disrepair. Various explanations were given if a site was not maintained: perhaps the extended family were not faithful Orthodox Christians, perhaps they did not have the money to maintain it, or perhaps they no longer lived in the area. I noticed that all the stones had a photo of the deceased, a birth date and death date with the exception of children. These sites were actually little plots, measuring different sizes depending on the number of families buried there. Sites that were well organized and maintained contained flowers, a gravestone, a metal fence surrounding it and grass or fine gravel as the "floor." Others (those whose family members had more money presumably) had rock or marble half-walls. In between grave plots there were small metal tables and stools meant to invite relatives to a shared meal with the deceased. Many sites contained old bottles that were left as gifts for the dead. It is said that when you bring water, wine, beer, etc., you must pour some on the grave and it "goes to them." I was told by one informant that tradition holds that the more you pour, the happier and more fulfilled the family member(s) are in the afterlife. Also, the bottles should be left at the gravesite and not removed. At a special time each year the grave site is cleaned, grass cut, more wine poured, prayers said, etc., and empty bottles are replaced and new put back (usually filled with liquid). It is common at many burials that dirt from the surrounding village be placed by the handful by the men of the family.

The above observations are well known both in oral and documented writings across the Orthodox world. For example a case can be made that much of Georgian Orthodox practices have been adopted and safeguarded from Byzantine times through Russian involvement and influence. Michel Bouchard has studied Russian Orthodox gravesite practices and much of what he describes also applies to the Georgian situation.[26] In his research he highlighted the funerary rites themselves along with the customary visitation days (second, third, ninth, twentieth, and fortieth days, and then one year after death) in which friends and relatives would visit graves and perform various rites.[27] All of these activities were seen as a way to support the deceased in the afterlife and to maintain a relational and communal connection with them.

26. Bouchard, "Graveyards," 345–62.
27. Ibid., 349–50.

More could be said about funerary rites and grave visitations. However, the purpose of this project is not so much to explain in detail what others like Bouchard and Ingram have already done elsewhere,[28] but to understand how displacement affects these religious practices and further to show how IDPs have expanded the fields of meaning of these practices in displacement. To do this I will now turn to IDPs' stories and testimonials.

COLLECTIVE GRIEF: IDPS IN DISPLACEMENT AND THE STORY OF TANGIZI[29]

I first met Tangizi in the city of Rustavi in 1998. In my visits to Georgia since then I have always connected with him and his wife over a meal. Tangizi was an IDP from Abkhazia who was forced to leave his village in 1992. After traveling by bus to Tbilisi, he and several friends from Abkhazia decided to go to Moscow and seek out other opportunities. Tangizi explained to me that he had relatives there who owned a business and that he and his parents decided that since his country was at war, he should seek a future in Russia. Life in Russia turned out to be very difficult for Tangizi and after several failed attempts at starting over, Tangizi decided to relocate to Georgia some years later where he met and married his wife Victoria and had three children.

In my interview with Tangizi, he told me that his parents had escaped from Abkhazia to Rustavi (the second largest city in Georgia) and settled there to live out their remaining years. He explained that a few years earlier his father had died in Rustavi and spoke about the most memorable aspects of the funeral. Since his father could not be buried in Abkhazia, Tangizi worked out a plan with his uncle in Abkhazia to bring a jar of dirt and sprinkle it on his fathers' grave. According to Tangizi, this action made his father very happy. Though sprinkling dirt on graves is a common practice in many cultures, this occasion was even more symbolic because of his father's desire to be buried in the home soil of Abkhazia. Though he could not be buried there, a jar of dirt would create a symbolic link to the homeland, even in death. He went on to explain that if Abkhazia ever opened back up for Georgians to return, that he would exhume his father's bones and rebury him there "like Moses who took

---

28. Ingram, "'The Dearly Not-Quite Departed.'"
29. Tangizi, interviewed by author, October 9, 2013.

Joseph's bones and reburied them."³⁰ He further explained that over one thousand people (IDPs from Abkhazia) attended his father's funeral—some he knew but most he did not.

That other IDPs from Abkhazia attended the funeral to honor Tangizi's deceased father despite not knowing him seemed important. By grieving for a man they knew only by virtue of his origins in Abkhazia, their grief was situated to simultaneously honor the homeland by honoring one of its members. Most of the grieving participants could not return to visit their own ancestral graves, but they could attend the funerals of their brethren in displacement. What was normally gathering of family and friends now became an IDP collective display of grief by and with "strangers" with undertones of solidarity (for the living-dead), survival (for the living-in-displacement), and remembrance of the Abkhazian homeland.

This phenomenon is not unlike the dynamics of grieving populations after the Balkan wars. In *The Political Lives of Dead Bodies*, Katherine Verdery attempts to rethink the politics of post-socialist/post-war nationalisms by looking at the meanings of cultural treasures like kinship systems, spirits, ancestor worship, and ultimately "dead body politics" that animate nation building.³¹ After the ethno-genocide perpetrated in various regions of the Balkans was over, mass funerals and reburials took place which re-inserted dead bodies in their "proper" ancestral soil. In Verdery's analysis reburial in native soil was required in order to avoid the negative effects of ancestors relations in death and served to set up a proper relationship with the community of the dead. Ultimately, for Verdery, the devotion to ancestors became regarded as a new nationalism, or the recovery of an old one in new ways.³²

In Tangizi's fathers' case, the similarities and differences are evident. Similarities are that in the process of burial, there is a collective honoring and memorial given to a distant homeland. Their remembering invoked both solidarity and protest given the contested state of affairs in Abkhazia. It signaled an identity of belonging to the Abkhazian homeland as well as a statement of belonging to each other in displacement. The differences, however, seem to lie in the fact that despite Verdery's analysis, Orthodox IDPs in Georgia did not view burial or reburial in Abkhazian soil in the

---

30. Tangizi, interviewed by author, October 6, 2013.
31. Verdery, *The Political Lives of Dead Bodies*, 41–42.
32. Ibid.

same way. They certainly did not view it as a possibility given restricted access; in the above example, Tangizi wanted to rebury his father's bones only if Abkhazia would be reopened to them. But most importantly, they did not view reburial in Abkhazian soil as a requirement to set up 'normal relations' with the dead in the afterlife. Rather what the Georgian situation reveals is a way of remembering the dead that allows for both a longing for a return to Abkhazia as well as the possibility to transfer that longing to their fellow Abkhazians in displacement, effectively expanding their ancestral lineages in their current place.

This dual possibility of remembrance, both as a longing for the past and an expansion of the present, is tied primarily to the mourning ritual and the way in which relational contact with the deceased works itself out in displacement. Given Kotthoff's observations above about the community of the dead being present and addressed (symbolized by photographs) among the mourning community, the mourning ritual sets in motion relational contact between the living and the dead that transcends *time and space*. So while devotion to homeland is manifest in collective grieving, the belief that the spirit of the dead lives on and can be honored at someone else's grave means that the physical space of a gravesite while important does not preclude other spaces from fulfilling the same role.[33] This means that in practice, the gravesites in Abkhazia have taken on secondary importance behind the belief that suitable locations for grief and remembrance lay not only in Abkhazia, but in any grave connected to an Abkhazian homeland lineage.

This later point seemed to reflect the attitudes of other participants in the study. Eka for example, could not visit her family's gravesites in Sokhumi; instead she said that in addition to going to church she went to her friend's funeral and gravesites to pay her respects there.[34] Another IDP, Iamze, described her belief that even though her father had died in Abkhazia, that she doesn't regard him as dead, since his spirit lives on.

---

33. Also important is the service of remembrance at the Orthodox Church. The service of remembrance is a formalized liturgy in which the priest prays a blessing upon all the deceased members of one's family according to a list of names that worshippers give him. Worshippers first write names of their deceased ancestors down on a piece of paper and then hand them to one of the priests. Depending upon the size of the church and the number of priests ministering, the names are read out loud in the presence of the gathered community with recitations of Scripture, blessings, and quotes from Christian tradition. The service is for all Orthodox believers, but holds special importance for IDPs.

34. Eka, interviewed by author, September 21, 2013.

Her testimony is especially salient in this regard. When I asked her about her ancestral graves, she said, "As a matter of fact, I can't go there (to the graves). So we go to the church ceremony for remembrance. And the priests told me that you don't need to go to the grave [In Abkhazia] in order to show respect, because the body dies and the spirit is everywhere."[35] Others I spoke to indicated that some of the older generation of relatives had died in displacement and so they simply went to their graves instead. In each of these cases, the graveyard practices of the living toward the dead expanded the field of both ancestral lineage (to include non-relatives) and the meaning of specific geographical locations to include non-Abkhazian sites for burial. Both of these accommodations were made possible by the Georgian Orthodox view of the community of the dead as it became applied to the situation of displacement.

GRAVEYARDS: SITES OF REMEMBRANCE

These observations within the context of displacement seem to support yet extend Bouchard's observations about the role of graveyards in the Orthodox world. He notes several important themes, each of which needs expanded in considering the effects of displacement upon gravesite rituals: 1) a ritual connection at gravesites, if maintained, charges the space with both sacred and nationalistic/ethnic significance; 2) graveyards serve a dual role: they are the homes of the dead and they mark out the "homeland" of the living; 3) that graveyards are a "home for the soul in death and a site of the future resurrection."[36]

On the first point, because visiting family graves in Abkhazia is no longer possible, IDPs have substituted the graves of other IDPs (both friends/non relatives and relatives) who have died in displacement as the primary site of remembrance. The ritual connection at gravesites in displacement continues to establish a sacred connection to ancestral heritage by virtue of mourning rituals. These connections have also been expanded to include other IDP lineages and constitute the means of survival and solidarity of IDP identity, as it is associated with the Abkhazian homeland. On Bouchard's second point above, the nature of displacement changes the apparent function of graves to mark out a specific longed-for homeland. Instead of an Abkhazian homeland, lost and no longer accessible, graves in displacement mark out new imaginative possibilities.

---

35. Iamze, interviewed by author, September 24, 2013.
36. Bouchard, "Graveyards," 361.

Whatever may come of the opportunity of return to Abkhazia, graves now in displacement make possible the expansion of the homeland to include Georgia proper and not only territory of Abkhazia. While Abkhazia remains the "true" homeland, graves in displacement, i.e. other parts of Georgia, mark out and expand a wider homeland.

On Bouchard's third point, displacement has contested or challenged the belief that graves are a home of the soul by allowing a refocusing on the "everywhere" of the spirit. Iamze's belief that the "body is in the grave, but the spirit is everywhere" reconfigures sacred space away from a specific homeland to potentially new places or, more accurately, any place. The spirit as "everywhere" is not held by time or place and places may mediate spiritual presence but are not dependent upon it.

CONCLUSION

I have argued that gravesites in displacement have changed the way IDPs remember their loved ones. The meaning attached to gravesites nevertheless remains deeply felt as the news article cited in the beginning of this chapter indicated. Not all IDPs are satisfied with these alterations of tradition as many continue to risk going back into Abkhazia.

Ultimately, the role of gravesites (in both belief and ritual practice) signals a contested space in displacement. They simultaneously remind mourners of their loss and yet open up possibilities for an expansion into new territories of the spirit. Graveyards by implication are symbolic of a complex field of meaning where they can signal both implacement and displacement at the same time. Low and Lawrence-Zuniga's observations are relevant here:

> [Contested places] are geographic locations where conflicts in the form of opposition, confrontation, subversion, and/or resistance engage actors ... While these conflicts principally center on the meanings invested in sites, or derive from their interpretation, they reveal broader social struggles over deeply held collective myths ... In this way contested spaces give material expression to and act as loci for creating and promulgating, countering and negotiating dominant cultural themes that find expression in myriad aspects of social life.[37]

As sites of contestation, graves serve to "create and promulgate" a complex imaginary of a longed for homeland and yet at other times

---

37. Low and Lawrence-Zúñiga, *The Anthropology of Space and Place*, 18.

open up the possibility of imagining new homelands. For some, the act of remembrance becomes a protest and a way to negotiate their displaced status and to safeguard the possibility (both real and imagined) of a return. In fact graves function not unlike other forms of social mechanisms of remembrance in Georgia today. As I discussed in Chapter 2, Ketevan Sulava documents so called Abkhazian IDP schools in exile, which serve to educate the generation of IDPs born in displacement about Abkhazia and to instill the desire to return.[38] Sulava as well as Kabachnik argue that IDPs generally resist integration in the localities where they find themselves in part because they do not want to give up on the hope of an eventual return, but also because of government policies aimed at the recovery of their homeland.[39]

At other times graves signal new possibilities by their very inaccessibility. The mourning rituals of IDP families at first glance show how IDP identity is transferred from individual family members to the larger IDP group. In this way they transfer their devotion to one another's dead in displacement as a way of collectivizing their religious identity and homeland longings (Tangizi's story above). Yet a deeper investigation also reveals that these same mourning rituals expand time and space categories and therefore open up new ways to reimagine the place of a gravesite and see the "everywhere of the spirit."

---

38. Sulava, "At the Crossroads of Identity."
39. Kabachnik et.al., "Where and When Is Home?," 318.

6

Theology in the Context of Displacement
The Iconic Frame of Borders, Homes, and Graves

UP TO THIS POINT, my purpose has been to describe some aspects of IDP faith and religious practices in forced displacement. While the location of their displacement is geographically situated in the republic of Georgia, sub-locations of displacement (borders, homes and graves) have emerged as powerful influencers for religious response. These sub-locations of displacement shape religious responses because they are storied places that hold together significant events, memories, and sacred experiences that have accumulated to create an identity in the world. I have described Christian responses as seeking to reconcile bordered spaces, remake homes with sacred connections from the past, and reimagine the space of gravesites. In other words, faith responses seek to reshape the places of displacement and signal a theologizing moment for IDPs.

This theologizing moment, rooted in Orthodox religious practices and theological tradition, serves to expand existing IDP literature which emphasizes socio-cultural factors to the exclusion of deeper and more complex spiritual factors. Using existing studies on Georgian IDPs, I pointed out in Chapter 2 that the nature of Georgian displacement was characterized by internal, multiple, and protracted dimensions. Furthermore, I speculated that these dynamics simply do not explain the full picture of IDP realities since their religious identities have been largely overlooked. This chapter argues that along with these existing designations, there is a fourth dimension which has come to light through ethnography, namely that displacement must be viewed in a theological way because of how IDPs understand and respond to it.

In order to establish that displacement must be viewed theologically, this chapter aims to demonstrate that religious responses to borders, homes, and graves may be considered as exercises in theologizing about place in displacement. As I mentioned in chapter 1, theologizing in the Eastern Orthodox context should be understood primarily as a liturgical discourse of and between God and humanity in the places where people dwell. In order to demonstrate this claim, this chapter will develop what I believe to be the fundamental theological insight stemming from responses of IDPs to displacement, that is, that the theology of the icon provides IDPs with an "iconic frame" for theologizing about place in displacement.

This chapter will be divided into two parts. In part one, I will establish the foundational significance of icons in Orthodox theology through a discussion of the Incarnation of Jesus. Within Orthodox incarnational theology the emphasis is upon the transformation of materiality that now mediates divine presence. This relationship is broadly conceived through three common metaphors in iconic thought: border, betweenness, and window. In part two of the chapter, I seek to show how these iconic metaphors in Orthodox theology inform and sustain local theologizing around borders, homes, and graves. I will consider each location separately and examine pertinent theological themes that emerge. I will describe Father Archil's mission at the border theologically, as the themes of Orthodox tradition inform and shape his actions. The icon is central in telling the story because it opens up a mystical reality which points to a metaphysical border between God and humanity, yet transcends it through the mystery of the incarnation. Both in the home and in displacement, IDPs' experience of God's presence may be conceptualized theologically and placially via the icon corner. Reimagining gravesites in displacement speaks of a new theological awareness especially as it relates to the understanding of the icon as a window through which to gaze and reimagine. The icon in both its theological and practical application is the core thread that runs through each location and characterizes a local or contextual theologizing in iconic frame.

THE CENTRALITY OF ICONS IN EASTERN ORTHODOX THOUGHT

Before proceeding, I would like to establish the importance and totalizing effect that the icon has upon local Orthodox theology and practice. Ernst Benz, a German theologian whose writing on the Eastern Church has been significant for Western audiences, opens his famous work *The Eastern Orthodox Church: It's Thought and Life* with a chapter on the Orthodox icon. He concludes his first chapter with the claim, "Orthodox theology holds up the icon as the true key to the understanding of Orthodox dogma."[1] Benz's claim is substantiated by Leonid Ouspensky, the famous iconographer of the Russian Orthodox Church, when he says, "The Church sees in its holy image (icons) not simply one of the aspects of Orthodox teaching, but *the expression of Orthodoxy in its totality* . . . "[2] As a result, Ouspensky emphatically claims, "It is absolutely impossible to imagine the smallest liturgical rite in the Orthodox Church without icons."[3]

According to Ouspensky, the icon's totalizing effect in Orthodox theology and practice is rooted foremost in the relationship between a sacred image and the Incarnation of the second person of the Trinity.[4] After briefly discussing the relationship between the incarnation and the materiality of the icon, I will then discuss the ways the incarnation opens the door to a symbolic nature of the icon in human experience through three metaphors. Taken together, these metaphors help illuminate the theological basis of IDP responses to borders, homes, and graves.

St. John of Damascus, in his *Three Treatises on the Divine Images*, represents the fullest attempt to locate the theology of the icon within the Incarnation. By God becoming human, and by the Invisible becoming visible in flesh, the Incarnation is a fundamental statement about the sacramentality of material objects. By sending his Son in the flesh, God thereby infused materiality with sacramental meaning and points toward the possibility of transforming the human condition in both its spiritual and material dimensions. Thus St. John says, "I do not adore matter, but I

---

1. Benz, *The Eastern Orthodox Church*, 19.
2. Ouspensky, *Theology of the Icon*, 10; emphasis mine.
3. Ibid.
4. Ibid., 58.

adore the Creator of matter, who became matter for me, inhabiting matter and accomplishing my salvation through matter."[5]

According to Ouspensky, St. John's defense of the use of icons hinges upon a contrast between the Old and New Testament's use of images. In the Old Testament, the Israelites were prohibited from making "graven images" because it would be idolatrous to portray the invisible God who had only declared himself through his word. Thus the prohibition meant that no creature or created thing could be used as an image for God. (See Deuteronomy 4:16–19).[6] The New Testament by contrast, contains the invisible God becoming visible in the flesh and communicating in both word *and* image. Thus St. John says, "It is clearly a prohibition (in the Old Testament) of representing the invisible God. But when you see Him who has no body become man for you, then you will make representations of His human aspect."[7] Thus the Orthodox Church through the ages has incorporated sacred images into its liturgical life believing that the Incarnation itself provided the basis of all other sacred art. Leonid Ouspensky concludes, "The Church declares that the Christian image is an extension of the divine incarnation, that it is based on this incarnation and that, therefore, it is the very essence of Christianity, from which it is inseparable."[8]

In Orthodox theology then, there is a tendency to utilize the icon as an overarching symbol for the relationship between the spiritual and material realms because the icon incorporates both into its existence. As a material image grounded in the theological reality of the incarnation, the icon in local religious practice becomes symbolic of a wide variety of material relationships parlayed out into various manifestations of creaturely existence. These include material places, and the histories of saints who have gone before the community of faith. As a spiritual image, the icon and its usage is understood as conveying larger spiritual realities that transcend current places and materialities and ultimately transforms them. To these metaphors and their descriptions I will now turn.

The following metaphors are spatially imagined ways to conceptualize the interrelationship between humanity, the spiritual realm, and the

---

5. Ibid., 55. Also see Louth, *Introducing Eastern Orthodox Theology*, 97. Original citation in *On Images* 1.16; translation in St. John of Damascus, *Three Treatises On the Divine Images*, 23.

6. Ouspensky, *Theology of the Icon*, 54–55.

7. Ibid., 51.

8. Ibid., 58.

material world. These three metaphors describe the icon as 1) a "borderland" of human existence; 2) an "in-between" space of heaven and earth; and 3) a "window" to heavenly realities.

According to Louth, humanity's creaturely existence is lived out at "the borderlands" between the spiritual and the material. This is the result he says of "belonging to two different realms that are brought together in his [man's] existence."[9] Louth argues that the interplay between the material and spiritual worlds corresponds to the dual nature of humanity and the dual nature of Christ. Just as the incarnation demonstrates the duality of the perfect God and perfect Man brought together in one Man, so too humanity is both a spiritual and material being whose purpose is to become one with God in salvation.[10]

The icon participates in and illumines this duality, and therefore it too occupies a borderland existence between the material and the spiritual. As such, the icon opens up the possibility of a mutual crossing, both of the saint to the viewer and the viewer to the image represented in the icon. The sacred image ultimately connects humanity to its true nature in Christ and is, according to Lossky and Oupensky, an "inalienable part" of the doctrine of salvation.[11] Whether the icon portrays Christ, the Virgin Mary, or any number of other saints, these holy ones all share in common a glorified state of union with God or *theosis* and facilitate the same in the viewer.

The borderland metaphor of the icon is interesting for our purposes because as I will show below, its theology informs Archil's mission of fashioning icon cases and opening churches. His attempt to reconcile the space of the borderland, in other words, is similar to the way the icon itself points toward the reconciliation of both spiritual and material realities through the saint depicted within it.

As a borderland of existence, it follows then that the icon functions in a second metaphorical sense in human experience. According to Louth, icons occupy an "in-between space" in Orthodox theology that "enable us to pass" from one realm to another. Icons are "in between" the transcendent realm and the earthly realm and occupy the "thin" place that is the transition point from one to the other. Practically speaking, according to Louth, the icon is the "visual and immediate way of designating

---

9. Louth, *Introducing Eastern Orthodox Theology*, 102.
10. Ibid.
11. Ouspensky and Lossky. *The Meaning of Icons*, 28.

the in-between ... we stand on one side, and on the other side are the figures or events depicted in the icons."[12] But the icon represents something much deeper, it is a carrier of a symbolic spiritual relationship, a microcosm of heavenly realities.[13]

One way this "in betweenness" of the icon is experienced by the Orthodox faithful is through the spatial construction and interior design of Orthodox churches. The spatial features of an Orthodox church, more than any other thing, serve to disseminate the theology of the icon into the practice and performance of the Orthodox worshipper. According to Pavel Florensky, the iconostasis, which is a screen of icons separating the center of the Orthodox church (or alter) from the gathering place of the people, is a symbol of the thin place that lies between heavenly and earthly realities. At the iconostas, the two worlds come together and everything within the church, culminating with the iconostasis "wall," act as "membranes" which "continually direct us (the worshipper) to the central kernal."[14] The whole church or temple is "Jacob's ladder, leading from the visible to the invisible, [but] the alter is already the place of the invisible, the area set apart from this world, separate, withdrawn, dedicated."[15] Thus the church itself is spatially arranged to draw attention to the icons standing "in between" the heavenly realm or inner chamber and the earthly realm.

As both a borderland and an "in-between" place, the icon is central to the worshipper's experience of divine realities within the Orthodox faith tradition. The icon naturally invites the viewer to participate in heavenly realities while standing on the earthly and material side. Michel Quenot can say with conviction that every orthodox worshipper is keenly aware of participating in the great family of saints so that even as one looks at the interior of the Church, covered with icons and frescoes, "you assuredly no longer feel alone."[16] Thus it is with this view toward participation and realization of divine realities while in the present, that the icon as a window takes its shape in Orthodox devotional practice.

As a window to the Kingdom, icons are like a "portal, open to the glory and beauty promised to us, a grandeur and beauty of which we

12. Louth, *Orthodox Theology*, 115.

13. Fortounatto and Cunningham, "Theology of the Icon," 136.

14. Florensky, *Iconostasis*, 59. Also see Antonova, *Space, Time, and Presence in the Icon*, 96–97.

15. Florensky, *Iconostasis*, 59.

16. Quenot, *The Icon*, 43.

receive a foretaste within the living experience of the Church."[17] In spiritual practice, the icon allows for clarity of spiritual sight that otherwise remains cloudy and foggy without it. Without such spiritual practice, we "fail to see this light-bearing kingdom; [and] most often, we fail even to assume that it exists, and therefore we only sense unclearly in our hearts the spiritual currents of what is really happening around us."[18] As a window, the icon allows heavenly realities to pass through its frame to the worshipper and invites worshippers to "gaze" through the window and experience it. Florensky says, "a window is a window because a region of light opens out beyond it . . . the window all by itself i.e., apart from its relationship to the light, beyond its function as carrier of light—is no longer a window but dead wood and mere glass."[19] Thus, as a window, the icon opens up a view to the heavenly kingdom, to eternity, to the eschaton, and to the reality that all of life is to be lived in view of this larger "iconic world." Andrew Louth says it like this:

> The icon does not stand alone; we do not understand it simply by understanding what it depicts and how it manifests it. Instead, we can only fully understand an icon by seeing it as part of an iconic world, a world whose symphonic harmony is established and manifest in the manifold relationships and reflections that link everything together.[20]

The last two metaphors of the "in-between" and "window" flow naturally from the icon being considered a borderland between heaven and earth. The borderland creates the conditions upon which life is lived in the in-between with the window of the icon allowing a glimpse of heavenly realities, the ultimate transformation of earthly realities. In a parallel way, IDPs encounter a bordered world with the resultant shape of life being lived "in between." They live life in the "between" states of being a permanent resident, a tourist, and a refugee. Their memory participates in an ideal past and reinforces a desire to return to their former lives. Their multiple relocations have the effect of producing and destroying hope. They are hopeful for permanence until they are forced to move again. Likewise their identities as IDPs fluctuate between isolation and belonging. Their group remembrance practices and collective longings

17. Ibid., 7.
18. Florensky, *Iconostasis*, 64.
19. Ibid., 65.
20. Louth, "Orthodoxy and Art," 167.

create distance and isolation from other Georgians; yet they desire to belong, to be understood, and to keep their hopes of a better future alive.

Within these earth-bound material realities, IDPs practice their faith with a view toward transforming and altering the displacement experience. These practices show that the icon is central to the way they negotiate displacement and constitutes a theological moment. In the following sections, I return to the places of displacement to demonstrate how a theology of icons informs responses to borders, homes, and graves. I argue that the responses to reconcile borders, remake homes, and reimagine the spaces of gravesites, are best understood theologically by an "iconic frame" that seeks to ultimately redeem the material aspects of displacement with heavenly realties.

THEOLOGIZING THE "ICONIC" BORDERLAND

In chapter 3 I described that Father Archil responded to the border region of Gali by seeking to reconcile the contested space. Now I would like to consider further how reconciliation works itself out in the iconic frame. As I will show, the iconic frame can be expanded to include not simply sacred images and cases, but larger and more prominent displays of materiality such as churches themselves.

By way of review, the reader will remember that Archil's crossborder mission protested the estranging effects of a border and at the same time provided a different (non-bordered) vision of the future. The border was initially constructed as a ceasefire line to halt violent provocations by both Georgians and Abkhazians. Its initial intention as a "safety zone" was short-lived, and it has continued to foster an environment of distrust, fear, and oppression. At the same time, the erosion of morality, which Archil cited many times (giving both Georgian and Abkhazian examples), had also led to the conditions upon which the border was constructed and maintained its grip on the hearts of people. For example, he noted that the Gali border region had become increasingly immoral and that Abkhazian youth did not want to talk about morality or going to church anymore.[21] Likewise, he accused Georgians of not "living their lives in front of God" as a factor which led to their displacement. The borderization of the landscape was therefore fueled by the erosion of the value of human life and morality. It had become a place of fragmentation

---

21. Father Archil, interviewed by author, September 23, 2013.

of human values, a place defined by a lack of human dignity, and a spiritually dark place.

To meet these challenges, Archil set out to show a new way of relating to both the border and the degradation of humanity that it fostered. The most obvious way he did this was through repeatedly crossing the border at his own risk, a form of protest and resistance in a politicized place, a sort of liturgical mission. Once he crossed the border, he furthered his mission through the ministry of confession. He acknowledged the psychological and spiritual challenges that stemmed from war crimes from both Georgians and Abkhazians and the need to address them. One of his main strategies was to be available to both groups for confession. He wanted to provide an opportunity for forgiveness and friendship to be re-extended to people who had lost loved ones and had turned on each other as a result of the war. Father Archil admitted that confession was difficult because of access, and had experimented with allowing his contacts at the border to confess through the medium of a cell phone. Despite the apparent success of cell phone confessions, Archil felt that it was better to be in personal contact for greater authenticity and also because of his suspicion that Abkhaz authorities constantly monitored cell phone usage.

Not only had the border fostered an environment where human life was under-valued, it had the secondary effect of engendering a certain vision of the future. As I discussed earlier, the vision for a separate Abkhazia was and continues to be entangled in geo-political affairs, a long and tumultuous history with Russian foreign policy in the region, and the politicization of ethnic difference. To meet these somewhat complicated challenges, Archil invoked through religious tradition a vision of unity predicated upon a shared Christian past and certain contours of Orthodox theology. For him, the hostile place of the border could only be met spiritually through a renewed imagination, the kind that Gillian Crow calls the Orthodox vision of wholeness, "a total vision of Christianity which cannot be compartmentalized."[22] The fragmented border had become a place wherein a new vision for life and faith was most needed.

Father Archil's mission to accomplish a reenvisioning of the local imagination was rooted in the theology of the icon. Archil's contextual theology supposed an "iconic frame" of the world and utilized

---

22. Crow et al., *Living Orthodoxy in the Modern World*, 9.

a combination of visual strategies (rooted in the sacred image and the church) meant to reconcile the border space.

Theological-Social Vision of Icon and Ecclesia

In chapter 3 I described the complexity around which Archil used icons as a strategy at the border including some of the ways his own story intersected with the story of the icon. From this social analysis, I would now like to develop further the theology of the iconic frame related to Archil's mission at the border. According to Paul Evdokimov, "the icon . . . is the vehicle of personal presence."[23] The icon is not for the purpose of worshipping the saint depicted but a vehicle for the saint, and by implication God, to come out to greet the viewer. The perspective, says Metropolitan Anastasoios, is from the "person in the picture toward the viewer" and not the other way around.[24] Theologically, it is to "grasp that God and the saints come out to greet us as if heaven is already here to enrich our everyday lives."[25] The movement of God and the saints outward from the icon is a movement established theologically in the incarnation of Jesus and brought about by the Holy Spirit. The icon is holy by participation in this movement and not holy in itself, says Brown; it is "a sacrament of Light where history is already drawn up into eternity."[26]

As I discussed earlier, the icon is by nature a *symbolic border* itself. It represents a space between the spiritual and the material, between the heavenly saints, and humanity's existence. As a "border-image," it allows the free flow of divine grace through the image to the viewer so that the viewer can participate in the life of the saints and the glory of God. For Archil, only an encounter with God through the icons would ultimately change the vision of a place like the border. Theologically speaking, if history is drawn up into eternity in the "light" of the icon, then it follows that little histories, such as the history of a nation, a border, and a people, may also be drawn up again into the eternal vision of wholeness as the presence of God is engaged.

Archil's mission can be further illuminated by the common phrase "when the icon returns to Ilory" first discussed in Chapter 3. There I established the connection between the saint's biography and place

23. Evdokimov, *The Art of the Icon*, 40.
24. Metropolitan Athanasios of Hercegovina, "The Eschata in our Daily Life," 39.
25. Ibid.
26. Quoted in Brown, *God and Enchantment of Place*, 41.

(geography) and its significance for imagining sacred space and homeland. With the *spatial/placial nature* of the iconic frame established, the implication is that as the icon is a vehicle of personal presence for the saint and God to enrich our everyday lives, the Ilory icon has implications for the future of Georgian-Abkhazian relations at the border. However the Ilory icon is itself displaced from its place of origin and the icon's displacement is symbolic of the IDP's displacement. Thus it follows, that the Ilory icon's return to its own place of origin in Abkhazia would potentially signal peace and the reconciliation of the border space.

The Invisible Made Visible

The theological vision of the iconic frame in drawing people to a new life at the border is further expanded by Archil's use of a second visual strategy to point toward a historical unity that existed long before the border was constructed. Related to the usage of the iconic frame as a symbol for border reconciliation, Archil likewise utilizes the restoration of reopened churches to make visible the invisible God. A full treatment of Orthodox ecclesiology is beyond the scope of this work.[27] For my purposes here I would like to appropriate the visibility/invisibility distinction of the church in the theological work of Sergei Bulgakov and understand Father Archil's actions in the border region in light of it.

In his discussion on the church, Sergei Bulgakov argues that the essence of the church is "a divine-human unity . . . the divine life, revealing itself in the life of the creature."[28] The Church according to Bulgakov has both an invisible quality—by which he means mysterious and sacramental—and a visible life, which is only experienced through a "spiritual vision" which Bulgakov calls faith. He says, "Everything in the Church is invisible and mysterious, it all surpasses the limits of the visible world; but still the invisible may become visible, and the fact that we may see the invisible is the very condition of the existence of the Church."[29]

The invisible made visible for Bulgakov happens as society reflects the image and mystery of God in Christ. As I discussed in chapter 3, one of Archil's strategies was to make visible the ruins of ancient churches destroyed at a period of history when Georgians and Abkhazians were

---

27. For a good treatment, see Bulgakov, *The Orthodox Church*. Also see Florovskiĭ, *Collected Works of Georges Florovsky*.

28. Bulgakov, *The Orthodox Church*, 12–13.

29. Ibid., 13.

together. Upon displaying these broken stones, Archil claimed that the Abkhazians would "realize that we belong together." Making visible the ruined stones would memorialize and indeed sacralize Abkhazian and Georgian relations under the mystery of God. Only the reminder of their sacred past would solidify good relations in the present.

Bulgakov asserts that both the Incarnation and the Trinity are foundational to human transformation. Through the Incarnation, human life is analogous to the inner workings of Trinitarian life. Just as the Trinity is an all-embracing unity, so humanity is an essential unity, "but this unity manifests itself in love and by love, and it exists by virtue of participation in the one divine life of the Church."[30] According to Dalmais, the church building is a "visible expression of the community that meets in it, and that community is built on the foundations of the Apostles and the bishops who succeed them, and of those great witnesses the martyrs, and the monks who are heirs to their prophetical mission."[31] In other words, the visible church brings together the invisible unity of society under God in a physical location dedicated to the working out of the spiritual vision. Looking at Archil's actions through the lens of his own Orthodox theological values reveals that in the re-opening of churches the potential for a new societal unity presents itself anew. And as these churches existed long before a border was constructed, both Georgians and Abkhazians could reconcile the recent politicization of difference, based upon an ancient commitment to a unified body of Christ in society. Only the unity that was founded upon ancient theological commitments would allow a reconciled people to emerge in the midst of the borderization of life.

For Archil, the space of the border elicits a theological response of unity demonstrated most aptly in the re-opening of the greatest symbol of unity—the Church. Because the church building itself is a symbol of the unity of heaven and earth, so its opening or re-opening demonstrates the possibility of a renewal of ethnic relations. Archil's commitment to work with both Georgians and Abkhazians to accomplish this purpose is a direct confrontation upon the contested nationalisms and competing historiographies that have eroded public confidence and created mistrust. Archil's ministry at the border then reveals that the symbol of a unified border is not to be found in a common ethnicity, or a common social history, but rests upon love for one another fostered and maintained by

---

30. Ibid.
31. Dalmais, *Eastern Liturgies*, 140.

participation in the divine life of the Church. The importance of rebuilding the church at the border is highlighted against this theological backdrop, for only in its rebuilding will the spiritual vision be restored enough to participate in its unity.

IN-BETWEEN HOMES: AN "ICONIC" THEOLOGY OF HOME

In addition to the border, the home was a second location where theological themes emerge in displacement. In chapter 4, I discussed at length the way IDPs conceptualized home and the way faith narratives were brought to bear on that conceptualization. That chapter demonstrated that religious practices provided continuity between the loss of home and its reconstruction in displacement. The reader will recall that in chapter two I discussed displacement in terms of being an "in-between" reality. I used existing literature to demonstrate that IDPs were in between isolation and integration, in between homes, and in between settlement and return. The internal, multiple, and protracted natures of their displacement each contributed to an ongoing sense of estrangement. This section continues to extend the 'in-between' metaphor into the idea of homes as a way of highlighting the theological dimension of displacement.

Using Andrew Louth's concept of the icon as occupying an "in-between" place between the material and spiritual worlds, I intend to parallel the "in-betweenness" of losing and finding home in the IDP experience with the "in-betweenness" of the theology of the icon. I will first argue that this parallel is made possible by viewing the home in some sense as an icon in itself—a place that belongs to another world (including a distant past), yet continues to speak through memory, artifact, and image, and the remaking of that image in displacement. Secondly I will discuss the ways that a theology of icons points to the ultimate hiddenness of God, and hence the inaccessibility of a full recovery of home-past, yet allows what is visible in the present to be made manifest. In other words, the in-betweenness of the theology of the icon is similar to an experience of the hiddenness of God in losing home, and the visibility of God in remaking home again.

Home as Icon

I have already discussed the way in which the icon locates the holy in and through materiality. The icon as "in-between" reality bridges the divine realm via the medium of wood and glass. The material is sacred due to its participation in that realm and not because the material itself is sacred. The physical place of the home works much in the same way as the icon because it too participates in and bridges both a heavenly and earthly reality.

In order to begin to understand the theological connection between God and home, it is important to note that the origins of Christian faith among IDPs belong primarily to discussion pertaining to the role of the home and family. It was in the home during childhood where Eka took the faith like she took her mother's milk. Home was the place of family identity and faith formation.[32]

Yet due to home's multiscalar nature, it is symbolic of other realms of existence including the nation itself, and in the case of Georgian IDPs, the territory of Abkhazia. As a multilayered symbol, the home signifies not only personal and family formation, but integrates religious, ethnic, and national histories that have become sacralized over time.[33] For example, home is integrated into the national and religious consciousness by its connection to divine generosity. Perhaps this is why a common story circulating in Georgia today has remained so durable over time. The story relates how when God was apportioning the earth out to various peoples, the Georgians arrived late because they were having a party. When God saw their joy at life, he gave them the land of Georgia that he had originally reserved for himself. For many IDPs both the home and the homeland has its origin in Divine generosity and God's own enjoyment.[34]

The most profound sacralization of home, and of God's participation in it, is seen in the lives of Georgian saints as they too operate in the "between" spaces of the homeland image. Much like war heroes who are constantly remembered for the way they acted courageously in the development of any nation, Georgian monks who have lived faithfully in the midst of persecution (Arab Conquests, Ottoman empire, or Atheistic Communism) or who died defending the Christian faith, have in a real sense fertilized the soil of the Georgian landscape with their blood. They are venerated both in heaven and in the home and thus operate in the in-between space of national identity and Christian faith. These insights naturally lead to the home becoming a sanctuary of sorts where daily prayers of guidance, protection and remembrance of God and saints take

---

32. Eka, interviewed by author, September 21, 2013.

33. Blunt, and Dowling. *Home*, 6. I am indebted to these authors for their use of the term "multiscalar."

34. Suny, *The Making of the Georgian Nation*, 3.

place. As a result, the home is perceived as the origin of personal and family faith and a location of divine encounter.

By virtue of the icon corner, the home becomes not only an extension of the church in society but a location made holy as it participates in divine realities. The subject of how God reveals himself in a particular location is a debate that goes beyond this work.[35] Some places seem to mediate the divine encounter more than others. For example an old church or a beautiful landscape often facilitates sacramentality. For God to be located implies that certain places or events help make his presence felt among worshippers. In *A Christian Theology of Place*, John Inge brings balance to the discussion by asserting that the sacramentality of place corresponds to God's action *and* human reaction in that location. Inge says, "The world in itself is not sacramental, because sacramentality is an event that involves action by God and a response by a unique human being."[36] Inge calls for a *relational* view of the "sacramental understanding of reality" where in any given location, "God has not only to reveal himself, but we must have the grace to perceive Him."[37]

This relational understanding of sacramentality and encounter culminates in the icon corner in the home. God's presence and activity via the icon helps illuminate the story of Tavila's icon corner that managed to survive the destruction of her home in Abkhazia. She said,

> I prayed again and I worshiped God when I saw that they had not touched the icon corner. I saw all the rooms broken and only this one corner was not touched. I was shocked at everything around me, but as soon as I saw that corner was untouched I felt a peace in my heart. So when I saw everything broken I thought for myself that whoever it was, they have the fear of God somewhere and that is why they did not touch it.[38]

According to Tavila's interpretation, the fear of God caused the intruders not to touch the icon corner. This reaction seemed to be the direct result of some sense of religious understanding of the sacramentality of sacred space. Presumably, behind the intruders' respect for the icon corner was some sense of communal or cultural religiosity, but more importantly for Tavila, it was God who was suppressing violence and destruction with

---

35. For a good overview, see Brown, *God and Enchantment of Place*, 37–83.
36. Inge, *A Christian Theology of Place*, 81.
37. Ibid.
38. Tavila, interviewed by author, September 30, 2013.

the power of his presence. Tavila's shock turned to peace when she sensed that God *via the icon corner* had stayed the hands of those bent on completely destroying her house. The survival of the icon corner and thus the memory of her home as a sacred place, demonstrates that the home itself is often considered from an iconic frame, and ultimately functions as a surviving icon that bridges both a heavenly realm and the realities of displacement. In some sense, Tavila insists through memory, that the home *is* the icon that will never be completely destroyed because it too participates in divine blessing and protection. Thus, when describing the in-betweenness she felt as she lived in multiple homes, the one unchanging reality was that the icon corner defines the home and locates God's presence within it. She said, "Everywhere I go [meaning every home she has ever lived in] I have this corner, because we have no way out from God."[39]

The Hiddenness and Visibility of God and Home

Like the icon, which operates between the hiddenness of heavenly realities and the visibility of earthly existence, yet touches both, God is both hidden and revealed in the process of losing and finding home again. On the one hand, his hiddenness refers to the mystery surrounding why displacement happened in the first place and why certain traumatic events happened as they did. Tsisi, an IDP from Sokhumi said that her greatest challenge of faith was the question of "Why God . . . Why was I a mother of eight whose child was killed . . . why did this happen to me in my life?"[40] On the other hand, God's hiddenness is also demonstrated in the mixture of despair and hope at the thought of a return to their original homes—a return that belongs only to God. One IDP expressed that she prayed for God every day to take them back.

> The only hope that I have is in God. He is the only one I rely upon. First of all, I thank God that today I am alive, for food, I also ask God to help us to return. You know, I hear the country and government keep talking about it, but after 20 years it gets harder and harder to believe in that. I don't think we'll go back really.[41]

---

39. Ibid.
40. Tsisi, interviewed by author, September 20, 2013.
41. Iamze, interviewed by author, September 24, 2013.

Iamze contrasts the reliance upon politicians with her reliance upon God. At the same time her faith for a return is harder and harder to maintain almost to the point of despair. God seems therefore both hidden in the way that the future is unknown and that the past is confusing.

Though God's ways seem hidden to many IDPs' perceptions of the past and future, they perceive that he reveals himself in the struggles of life daily through images, saints, and encounters. At the beginning of the Introduction, I told a story about Iamze's dream wherein God warned her and prepared her for the war. Likewise, Eka's story about God delivering the two girls thought to have died in the bogs points to both his hiddenness and his presence. It is interesting that as I pressed for an explanation of Eka's story, she believed that the figure who guided the two girls to safety was a saint, the one she venerated in her icon corner. Furthermore, I recall how Tavila's testimony about how St. Nicholas wanted to bless her life and future exemplifies God's mediated presence through the intervention of an icon saint; and finally, Tsisi's conviction that God was providing for them everyday points to God's availability now. Speaking of her confidence in God she says,

> God is my right hand. He is everything for me ... that's it. I forgot about the joyful moments in my life, and sometimes I am thinking and wondering, "I don't have money what am I going to do tomorrow?" [She begins to cry] God somehow provides. You open up your eyes, you wake up, and something is fixed. I have two disabled kids that are alive ... God's hand is in that.[42]

What can be learned about God in view of IDP conceptualizations of home-loss and their pursuit of finding home again? First, God attends to the IDP experience by virtue of his presence. In an iconic frame, IDP encounters with God in displacement seem to move back and forth between experiencing the interplay of his transcendence on the one hand and his imminence on the other. His imminence for example often corresponds to an intimate memory of home, a placial awareness and even placial attachment. God is identified with the origins of faith in the home and in the gift of land and landscape. God is experienced in the home by way of the icon corner, a place that exists as a reminder that "there is no way out from God."[43] God is experienced as immanently present in the rituals of homemaking, hospitality, worship, prayer, and remembrance;

---

42. Tsisi, interviewed by author, September 20, 2013.
43. Tavila, interviewed by author, September 30, 2013.

all rituals which reinforce his presence with his people in and toward certain places. Yet experiencing God in displacement reminds IDPs that God is also transcendent. The inability to fully touch "home" as it was and the inaccessibility of distance creates less than full participation in the homeland imaginary. Just as the icon operates in the in-between spaces of heaven and earth, and does not in and of itself participate fully in God's essence, so the experience of God and home operate in similar ways.

THEOLOGIZING THE PLACE OF GRAVES IN THE ICONIC FRAME

In the same way that borders and homes have opened up ways of thinking theologically about place in displacement, gravesites too demonstrate how local actors theologize the significance of mourning rituals and gravesite loyalties for their everyday lives. I pointed out in chapter 5 that gravesites are among the most significant sites of devotion due to their connectivity with both the land and the afterlife. They mark out and embody the homeland and they are locations where the future resurrection will occur; they are therefore symbolic of the culminating hope of Christian theology and the continuation of the nation.

The inability of IDPs to freely return to graves of their family members only exacerbates their devotion and longing. Though some still risk going back to graves in secret, most do not. Adaptive strategies include an emphasis upon the importance of prayer for the deceased, participating in services of remembrance at local churches, and attending the gravesites of other IDPs. As I argued in chapter 5, these adaptations allowed an expansion of lineage and territory and most important for theology, the opening up of what Iamze referred to as the everywhere of the spirit.[44]

In the following, I would like to apply the iconic frame, the interplay of the material and spiritual as expressed in the theology of icons, to the way gravesite adaptations are considered. These adaptations seem to imply that when places of devotion (i.e. graves) are restricted from visitation and participation, local theologizing in the iconic frame calls for new ways of viewing old places to emerge and new places of devotion to take root. To put it another way, when a place is restricted there becomes an emphasis upon the *spirit* of place. That is, the emphasis is upon the freedom of the spirit to transcend the material form of the grave itself. Local Orthodox priests ministering to IDP populations have emphasized this

---

44. Iamze, interviewed by author, September 24. 2013.

as well. They encourage services of remembrance at church and prayers to be said instead of visiting graves. When Tavila says, "the grave is not important, prayer is the most important" she is not denying the symbolic importance of a bodily resurrection or the continued significance of graves for religious devotion. In fact, she is reinforcing the foundation of the iconic frame. Indeed she wants to emphasize that prayer is not contained or only effective *vis-à-vis* the original location (or material reality) but that its effectiveness transcends place ultimately because God transcended place in Christ's resurrection.

On the other hand, the iconic frame demands that materiality is maintained, because God has chosen to display his presence through it. And so local theologizing calls for new places of devotion to take root and replace those that are no longer accessible. This happens in two distinct ways in the Georgian context. First, as I have discussed before, IDPs transfer place-devotion to the graves of other IDPs. In many ways, they expand their lineage to include all those who have died in displacement and their remembrance of both the dead and the homeland is reinforced and rooted *in the new location*. Secondly, for many IDPs the service of remembrance at the church becomes a place of devotion that takes the place of the old gravesite location. In this regard Iamze says, "I can't go there [the gravesites] so I go to the church for the service of remembrance."[45] At this service, the names of her dead relatives are given to the priest for prayer and liturgical readings about the resurrection and life after death.

In sum, the iconic frame demands that with regard to the old graves, there is an emphasis upon the *spirit* of place. In the new places of devotion (graves in displacement and churches), there is an emphasis upon the *place* of the spirit—the new or alternate location where religious and cultural identity are safeguarded and maintained. Both dynamics reflect the iconic frame, and represent the devotionally rooted interplay between the spiritual and material in displacement as applied to key places. Though the physical space of family graveyards cannot be accessed, other material sites (graves, churches) can be, and these are the ways in which the material and spiritual relationship are maintained in displacement. In all these substitutionary places, the spiritual light that is part of the reality of the resurrection is experienced through the material realm. Both dynamics are at work and both are a product of local theologizing that re-imagines the relationship between spirit and the place of the gravesite.

45. Ibid.

Returning to the metaphor of a window, just as the icon opens up to the worshipper a world beyond and a new spiritual clarity, so graves operate in a similar fashion because in both instances, they open the participant to another way of viewing the world by seeing within it, yet beyond it.[46] Reimagining the place of gravesites in the iconic frame means that one's view of gravesite obligations is not the final reference point for life. Just as the window does not reference itself, but allows one to see the light on the other side, so gravesites are not the final end, but only the pathway or the view-way through to a renewal of history in the light of eternity. Like the icon, the graves represent materiality, which can be transferred to other material places through which to experience divine life and comfort. This may partially explain why IDPs can transfer devotion from one gravesite to another, even among non-biological family members. Their lineage expands itself into the realm of all those who have gone before and remain on the other side of the "window" as it were. At the same time, with Tavila, reimagining gravesites from the iconic frame led to the opening up of the "everywhere of the spirit" a phrase as much about how prayer operates as it is about the eschatological reality of the resurrection to be experienced now.

To summarize, the purpose of this chapter is to establish that Georgian IDPs respond to displacement in a theological way through looking at borders, homes, and graves through the iconic frame. The iconic frame is brought about by the diffusion of the theology of icons into everyday life in displacement. Icons are utilized at the border, in the homes, and at gravesites, yet because they are carriers of symbolic realities, these very locations become part of an "iconic world" and viewed as such. Just as the icon points toward heavenly realities and participates in them now, borders, homes, and grave are ultimately redeemable through their materiality. The chapter also serves to demonstrate that displacement must be understood beyond its internal, multiple, and protracted dimensions and into a theological realm where the icon both explains and sustains attempts to transform the places of displacement.

---

46. See Quenot, *The Icon*.

Conclusion

The Displaced Gaze

THIS STUDY SET OUT to explore the dynamics of a lived faith in the Georgian context of displacement as a demonstration and description of a local theologizing process. Theologizing in the Eastern Orthodox context, understood as a liturgical discourse between God, people, and places, relates to the distinct ways religious understanding and practices are directed toward borders, homes, and graves. In each place, a local or contextual theology emerged that sought to reconcile, remake, and reimagine these places through the iconic frame. Such a process implies that displacement is a distinct source location for understanding an embodied theology.

Because displacement fundamentally means "out of place" with regard to one's orientation in and toward the place-world, the study first required a closer look at the concept of place and its importance in human life. Life lived "out of place: led to a discussion of displacement's primary characteristics as internal, multiple, and protracted. I pointed out from the literature that internal displacement, defined as displaced within one's own national borders, holds increasingly complex challenges for integration and return. On the one hand, IDPs, along with their fellow Georgians, contest their own integration into mainstream society. On the other, a partial return to Gali comes with its own challenges of belonging and identity. The multiple and protracted dimensions of displacement also add to the long-term insolvability of the crisis in Georgia, a crisis often exacerbated by government policies toward Abkhazia. Forcibly relocated time and again, IDPs truly are a people living "in-between" the various dimensions of being in place and out of place.

From this macro-societal perspective, I next sought to understand through life-stories of IDPs the dynamics of religious response to displacement. The study revealed a set of contested places (borders, homes, graves) that highlighted and reinforced the displacement experience. These places shape religious responses, yet these responses also reshape these place-imaginaries through the Orthodox theology of the icon.

All of this implies the larger purpose of the book: while the broader literature on Georgian IDPs provides helpful conceptual dimensions to displacement, i.e. internal, protracted, and multiple; these categories tend to obfuscate a powerful religious identity at work in Georgian IDPs. And while they provide crucial explanations of socio-cultural, psychological, and geopolitical realities within which ordinary Georgian Christians experience life, they are nevertheless incomplete without attention to how religious attitudes signal a theologizing moment for IDPs.

Fundamentally then, the study concludes that the displacement experience is best understood theologically through the iconic frame. Another way to clarify theology done in this way is to utilize the terminology of icon-gazing from popular religious practice. Gazing in the Orthodox sense is a two-way encounter with the saint where the saint gazes and the viewer gazes back.[1] It is spiritual exercise of the heart and mind whereby the participant looks intently into the eyes of the icon to behold the beauty of transfiguration and participate in the saint's holiness. Each icon is inspired in such a way that certain features come to light. Jim Forrest's popular study on Saint Nicholas the Wonderworker is insightful in this regard. After describing Nicholas's upbringing and calling, Forrest describes St. Nicholas's life as "tireless in his care of people in trouble or need."[2] He locates these characteristics in St. Nicholas's face on the icon itself. He says, "The icons of Saint Nicholas are usually full-face views in which we glimpse his kindness, his attentiveness, and his strength of faith."[3]

Doing local theology within the iconic frame may be considered a type of "displaced gaze" which gathers together the histories and biographies of people and places and sees in and beyond them into the reality of the kingdom of God with expectant hope. In this sense, the displaced gaze may be considered synergistically, as that "light" from a future hope

---

1. Kenna, "Icons in Theory and Practice," 356.
2. Forrest, *Praying with Icons*, 152.
3. Ibid., 152.

operating within local agents to *replace and reshape* existing realities. The displaced gaze operates at the borderland of past and future longing; at the in-betweenness of being at home on earth as it will be in heaven, and sees through the window of the iconic frame the true light which will eventually lead to a new world.

In each of these 'iconic frames', the displaced gaze reconciles, remakes, and reimagines present experiences with future, more hopeful realities. Just as an icon in itself is only material wood and glass without the greater reality to which it points; borders, homes, and graves are made to be more than political or social problems to be solved. They are more than the pain of loss that they represent, and more than a social agenda on the minds of IDPs. Rather, like the icon, these places are "view-ways" through to a greater and more substantive reality; a reality that facilitates local agency as the believer participates in them through the theology of the iconic frame.

In concluding this project, I would like to relate the importance of a theological understanding of displacement not only to local IDP literature, but to the broader field of migration and theology. First, this study can serve to provide a model of the significance of a theologically informed reading of migrant/refugee life and faith connected to the larger tradition of Eastern Orthodoxy. As such, this study aligns with other attempts (namely, Cruz and Nagy referred to in chapter one) to situate theology at the nexus of socio-cultural (including globalizing) processes and lived Christian faith. This means that displacement, like migration, can likewise hold value for theologians because of the ways believing Christians articulate their faith experience within it. One result, as Groody implies in his work among Latino migrants, is pastoral awareness and a deeper appreciation of the inner geography of the heart to which these migrants map out their exterior journeys.[4]

In addition, the study proposes that key places shape and are shaped by religious identities and theological realities. For instance, the local theology of Orthodox IDPs in Georgia adds to global conversations about the relationship between faith, migrant identity, and longings for home. With increasing attention given to diaspora networks, transnational migration flows, and return migrations, it is important to read these phenomena in theologically constructive ways. How one conceptualizes the determination to remake home in the present is crucial for a holistic

---

4. Groody, "The Spirituality of Migrants."

understanding. For example, Heidi Armbruster argues that home among Syrian Christian migrants is a "transnational mode of identity" with a tension between home as one's *roots*, and home as one's *routes*.[5] In the Georgian context of displacement, home may also be understood in this way.[6] However, a closer look at IDP religious practices reveal that home is also theological—understood as a mode of religious and national identity articulated and reinforced within the iconic frame of Georgian Orthodox theology.

Once again, we return to the importance of theology. An analysis of a local theological perspective clarifies, illuminates, and must inform a comprehensive understanding of migrant or refugee faith. In other words, a theological reading of the displacement experience is as important as any other social, cultural, or geo-political observation that a wider academic community can provide. Without a theological understanding of displacement, sourced in IDP testimonials and resourced by local theological tradition, the complexity of migrant/refugee faith and displacement in its other forms diminishes accordingly.

---

5. Armbruster, "Syrian Christians in Turkey and Germany," 32.

6. For example Kabachnik conceptualizes "home as a journey" to describe IDP imaginings of home. See Kabachnik, Regulska, and Mitchnek, "Where and When is Home?," 317.

Appendix A

Maps of the Gali Region and of Abkhazia

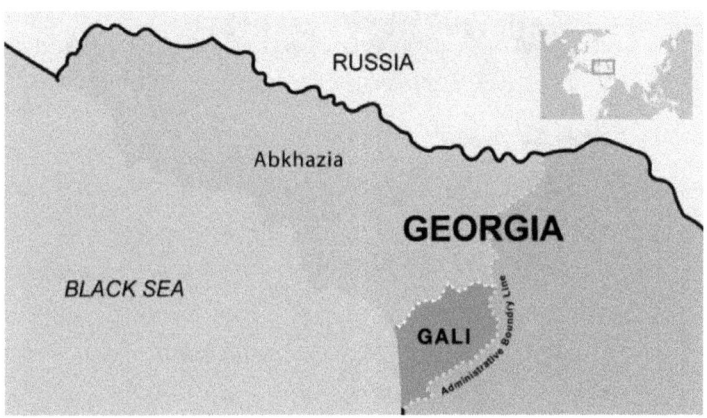

Appendix A

Appendix B

Life Narrative Interview Questions

ABKHAZIA - LIFE SITUATION

- Where were you born? Which city?
- Who was in your family? Tell me about your parents
- How many brothers and sisters did you have?
- What kind of house did you grow up in?
- Did your parents own their land?
- What is your favorite memory about your home in Abkhazia/Ossetia?
- Did you have good relationships with your neighbors?
- What was life like back before the war?
- Did you attend the Orthodox Church in your town?

MOVE FROM ABKHAZIA/SOUTH OSSETIA

- When did you leave Abkhazia/South Ossetia? Where did you go first?
- How many times have you moved since the war?
- What was something that you brought with you when you moved?

INTERNAL DISPLACEMENT NOW

- Do you own/rent your home?

- What does it take to make a new life here in this place?
- Even though it is different than your former house, how do you make this house your home?
    - o Tell me about your wall décor (pictures, material objects)
    - o What do you like to show people who come and visit? Why is it important to you?
    - o What do you wish was different about this place/home?
    - o What would you change if you could?
- What has been one of your greatest challenges since being displaced?

IDP AND FAITH

- How did you experience God growing up? How do you experience God now in displacement?
- Can you tell me a time when you felt that God was very near to you? When he was distant?
- Do you have a bible? An Icon? If so, which one? Why is this Icon important to you in displacement?
- Do you feel that you have learned anything new about God since moving here, since being an IDP?
- When do you feel closest to God now? When do you feel farthest away?
- Tell me about how the Orthodox Church has helped you as an IDP.
- What are your hopes for the future?

Bibliography

Abashidze, Zaza, et al. *Witness through Troubled Times: A History of the Orthodox Church of Georgia, 1811 to the Present.* London: Bennett & Bloom, 2006.
Adams, Nicholas, and Charles Elliott. "Ethnography Is Dogmatics: Making Description Central to Systematic Theology." *Scottish Journal of Theology* 53 (2000) 339–64.
Allen, W. E. D. *A History of the Georgian People: From the Beginning Down to the Russian Conquest in the Nineteenth Century.* New York: Barnes & Noble, 1971.
Athanasios of Hercegovina. "The Eschata in our Daily Life." In *Living Orthodoxy in the Modern World: Orthodox Christianity & Society*, edited by Andrew Walker, and Costa Carras, 37–49. Crestwood, NY: St. Vladamir's Seminary Press, 2000.
Anderson, Benedict. *Imagined Communities: Reflections on the Origin and Spread of Nationalism.* London: Verso, 2006.
Anderson, Tony. *Bread and Ashes: A Walk through the Mountains of Georgia.* London: Cape, 2003.
Antonova, Clemena. *Space, Time, and Presence in the Icon: Seeing the World with the Eyes of God.* Farnham: Ashgate, 2010.
Armbruster, Heidi. "Syrian Christians in Turkey and Germany." In *New Approaches to Migration? Transnational Communities and the Transformation of Home*, edited by Nadje Al-Ali and Khalid Koser, 17–33. London: Routledge, 2002.
Balzer, Marjorie Mandelstam. *Religion and Politics in Russia: A Reader.* New York: Sharpe, 2010.
Basso, Keith H. *Wisdom Sits in Places: Landscape and Language among the Western Apache.* Albuquerque: University of New Mexico Press, 1996.
Benz, Ernst. *The Eastern Orthodox Church: Its Thought and Life.* Garden City, NY: Anchor, 1963.
Berdahl, Daphne. *Where the World Ended: Re-Unification and Identity in the German Borderland.* Berkeley: University of California Press, 1999.
Blunt, Alison, and Robyn M. Dowling. *Home.* London: Routledge, 2006.
Bouchard, Michel. "Graveyards: Russian Ritual and Belief Pertaining to the Dead." *Religion* 34 (2004) 345–62.
Bouma-Prediger, Steven, and Brian J. Walsh. *Beyond Homelessness: Christian Faith in a Culture of Displacement.* Grand Rapids: Eerdmans, 2008.
Brown, David. *God and Enchantment of Place: Reclaiming Human Experience.* Oxford: Oxford University Press, 2004.
Bruns, Bettina, and Judith Miggelbrink. *Subverting Borders: Doing Research on Smuggling and Small-Scale Trade.* Wiesbaden: VS, 2012.

Bulgakov, Sergiĭ. *The Orthodox Church*. Crestwood, NY: St. Vladimir's Seminary Press, 1988.

Casey, Edward S. *Getting Back into Place: Toward a Renewed Understanding of the Place-World*. Bloomington: Indiana University Press, 2009.

Campese, G. "The Irruption of Migrants: Theology of Migration in the 21st Century." *Theological Studies* 73 (2012) 3–32.

Charles, Robia. *Religiosity and Trust in Religious Institutions: Tales from the South Caucasus (Armenia, Azerbaijan and Georgia)*. Berkeley Program in Eurasian and East European Studies. eScholarship, University of California, 2009. http://www.escholarship.org/uc/item/1b88b59g.

Clendenin, Daniel. *Eastern Orthodox Christianity: A Western Perspective*. Grand Rapids: Baker Academic, 2003.

Clingerman, Forrest. "Interpreting Heaven and Earth: The Theological Construction of Nature, Place, and the Built Environment." In *Nature, Space, and the Sacred: Transdisciplinary Perspectives*, edited by Sigurd Bergmann et al., 45–54. Farnham, UK: Ashgate, 2009.

Cohen, Roberta, and Francis Mading Deng. *Masses in Flight: The Global Crisis of Internal Displacement*. Washington, DC: Brookings, 1998.

Corso, Molly "Georgia: For IDPs, Orthodox Easter Reinforces Pain of Separation." *Eurasianet*, April 16, 2012. Accessed December 2013. http://www.eurasianet.org/node/65271.

Creet, Julia, and Andreas Kitzmann. *Memory and Migration: Multidisciplinary Approaches to Memory Studies*. Toronto: University of Toronto Press, 2011.

Cruz, Gemma Tulud. *An Intercultural Theology of Migration: Pilgrims in the Wilderness*. Leiden, Boston: Brill, 2010.

Chrysostom, John. "On the Cemetery's Name and the Cross." Accessed February 2015. http://www.johnsanidopoulos.com/2011/05/st-john-chrysostoms-homily-on-cemetery.html.

Dalmais, Irénée. *Eastern Liturgies*. New York: Hawthorn, 1960.

Davies, Douglas James. *Death, Ritual and Belief: The Rhetoric of Funerary Rites*. London: Continuum, 2002. http://ezproxy.asburyseminary.edu/login?url=http://search.ebscohost.com/login.aspx?direct=true&db=cat00591a&AN=aslc.47716497&site=eds-live.

De Coulanges, Fustel. *The Ancient City: A Study on the Religion, Laws, and Institutions of Greece and Rome*. Garden City, NY: Doubleday, 1956.

Dunn, Elizabeth Cullen. "The Chaos of Humanitarian Aid: Adhocracy in the Republic of Georgia." *Humanity: An International Journal of Human Rights, Humanitarianism, and Development* 3, no. 1 (2012) 1–23. http://muse.jhu.edu/journals/humanity/toc/hum.3.1.html.

Evdokimov, Paul. *The Art of the Icon: A Theology of Beauty*. Redondo Beach, CA: Oakwood, 1990.

Ferris, Elizabeth, ed. *Resolving Internal Displacement: Prospects for Local Integration*. Washington, DC: Brookings Institution-London School of Economics, Project on Internal Displacement, June 2011.

Fiddes, Paul. *Seeing the World and Knowing God : Hebrew Wisdom and Christian Doctrine in a Late-Modern Context*. Oxford: Oxford University Press, 2013.

Florenskii, Pavel. A. *Iconostasis*. Crestwood, NY: St. Vladimir's Seminary Press, 1996.

Florovskiĭ, G. *Collected Works of Georges Florovsky. An Eastern Orthodox View*. Belmont MA: Nordland, 1972.

Forrest, Jim. *Praying with Icons*. Maryknoll NY: Orbis, 2008.

Foucault, Michel, and Jay Miskowiec. "Of Other Spaces." *Diacritics* 16, no. 1 (1986) 22–27.

Frichova, Magdalena. *Displacement in Georgia: IDP Attitudes to Conflict, Return and Justice*. London: Conciliation Resources, 2011.

———. "Participation of Persons Belonging to National Minorities—Cases of Samtskhe-Javakheti and Gali." *International Journal on Minority and Group Rights* 16, no. 4 (2009) 643–51.

Garces-Foley, Kathleen. *Death and Religion in a Changing World*. Armonk, NY: Sharpe, 2006.

Geertz, Armin W., and Jeppe Sinding Jensen. *Religious Narrative, Cognition, and Culture: Image and Word in the Mind of Narrative*. Sheffield, UK: Equinox, 2011.

GeoStat.Ge. "Population." National Statistics Office of Georgia. Accessed March 2014. http://geostat.ge/?action=page&p_id=1184&lang=eng.

Gertsmava, Nino. "Housing Hopes Dim for Georgia's Refugees." Institute for War and Peace Reporting, 4 March 2013, CRS Issue 678. Accessed 13 February 2015. http://www.refworld.org/docid/5135f5391e85b3f.html.

Gill, Robin. *Theology in a Social Context*. Farnham, UK: Ashgate, 2012.

Groody, Daniel G. "Crossing the Divide: Foundations of a Theology of Migration and Refugees," *Theological Studies* 70, no. 3 (2009) 638–67.

Groody, Daniel G. "The Spirituality of Migrants: Mapping an Inner Geography." In *Contemporary Issues of Migration and Theology*, edited by Elaine Padilla and Peter C. Phan, 139–56. New York: Palgrave Macmillan, 2013.

Groody, Daniel G., and Gioacchino Campese. *A Promised Land, a Perilous Journey: Theological Perspectives on Migration*. Notre Dame: University of Notre Dame Press, 2008.

Hanganu, Gabriel. "Eastern Christians and Religious Objects." In *Eastern Christians in Anthropological Perspective*, edited by Chris Hann and Hermann Goltz, 33–55. Berkeley: University of California Press, 2010.

Hann, Chris, and Hermann Goltz. "Introduction, The Other Christianity?" In *Eastern Christians in Anthropological Perspective*, edited by Chris Hann and Hermann Goltz, 1–29. Berkeley: University of California Press, 2010.

Hewitt, George B. *Discordant Neighbours: A Reassessment of the Georgian-Abkhazian and Georgian-South Ossetian Conflicts*. Leiden: Brill, 2013.

Human Rights Watch. *Living in Limbo: The Rights of Ethnic Georgian Returnees to the Gali District of Abkhazia*. 15 July 2011. Accessed 7 January 2014, http://www.refworld.org/docid/4e270d032.html.

Inge, John. *A Christian Theology of Place*. Aldershot: Ashgate, 2003.

Ingram, Anne Marie. "'The Dearly Not-Quite Departed: Funerary Rituals and Beliefs about the Dead in Ukrainian Culture.'" PhD diss., University of Virginia, 1998. http://search.proquest.com.ezproxy.asburyseminary.edu/docview/304458508?accountid=8380.

International Crisis Group. *Abkhazia: The Long Road to Reconciliation*. Brussels: International Crisis Group, 2013. Accessed June 18, 2018. https://www.crisisgroup.org/europe-central-asia/caucasus/abkhazia-georgia/abkhazia-long-road-reconciliation 2013.

Iskander, Fazil'. *Sandro of Chegem*. New York: Vintage, 1983.

Kabachnik, Peter. "Shaping Abkhazia: Cartographic Anxieties and the Making and Remaking of the Abkhazian Geobody." *Journal of Balkan and Near Eastern Studies* 14, no. 4 (2012) 397–415.

———. "Wounds That Won't Heal: Cartographic Anxieties and the Quest for Territorial Integrity in Georgia." *Central Asian Survey* 31, no. 1 (2012) 45–60.

Kabachnik, Peter, Joanna Regulska, and Beth Mitchneck. "Where and When Is Home? The Double Displacement of Georgian IDPs from Abkhazia." *Journal of Refugee Studies* 23, no. 3 (2010) 315–36.

Kenna, Margaret E. "Icons in Theory and Practice: An Orthodox Christian Example." *History of Religions* 24, no. 4 (1985) 345–68.

Khan, Asif, and Khatia Odzelashvili, "A Profile of Conflict Induced Internally Displaced Persons (IDPs) of Telavi, Georgia: A Study Undertaken by Caucasus Peace Forum." Ottawa, ON: Caucasus Peace Forum, 2012.

King, Charles. *The Ghost of Freedom: A History of the Caucasus*. Oxford: Oxford University Press, 2008.

Lane, Belden C. *Landscapes Of The Sacred: Geography and Narrative In American Spirituality*. Baltimore: Johns Hopkins University Press, 2002.

Lang, David Marshall. *The Georgians*. New York: Praeger, 1966.

Larson-Miller, Lizette. "Roman Catholic, Anglican, and Eastern Orthodox Approaches to Death." In *Death and Religion in a Changing World*, edited by Kathleen Garces-Foley, 93–121. Armonk, NY: Sharpe, 2006.

Lefebvre, Solange, and Luiz Carlos Susin. *Migration in a Global World*. London: SCM, 2008.

Lester, Andrew D. *Hope in Pastoral Care and Counseling*. Louisville: Westminster John Knox, 1995.

Losi, Anne-Sophie, and Tamar Tavartkiladze. *A Heavy Burden: Internally Displaced in Georgia: Stories of People from Abkhazia and South Ossetia*. Universitäts- und Landesbibliothek Sachsen-Anhalt Genf: Internal Displacement Monitoring Centre, 2008. Accessed January 8th, 2014. http://www.internal-displacement.org/idmc/website/resources.nsf/%28httpPublications%29/9B7573E88B99BCE8C125743B003D5CA7?OpenDocument.

Louth, Andrew. *Introducing Eastern Orthodox Theology*. Downers Grove IL: InterVarsity, 2013.

———. "Orthodoxy and Art." In *Living Orthodoxy in the Modern World*, edited by Andrew Walker and Costa Carras, 159–77. Crestwood NY: St. Vladimir's Seminary Press, 1996.

Low, Setha M., and Denise Lawrence-Zúñiga. *The Anthropology of Space and Place: Locating Culture*. Malden, MA: Blackwell, 2003.

Lussi, Carmem "Human Mobility as a Theological Consideration." In *Migration in a Global World*, edited by Solange Lefebvre and Luis Carlos Susin, 49–60. London: SCM, 2008.

Machitadze, Zakaria. *Lives of the Georgian Saints*. Platina, CA: St. Herman of Alaska Brotherhood, 2006.

Mitchneck, Beth, Olga V. Mayorova, and Joanna Regulska. "'Post'-Conflict Displacement: Isolation and Integration in Georgia." *Annals of the Association of American Geographers* 99, no. 5 (2009) 1022–32.

Mitchneck, Beth, and Julia Carboni, "How Dynamic Is the Structure of Employment and Well-Being: A Comparison of IDPs from Abkhazia in the 1990's and South Ossetia in 2008." Paper presented at the Living in Displacement Conference, Tbilisi, Georgia, March 2011. Accessed February 2015. http://georgia.idp.arizona.edu/docs/IDP%20Well-Being%20Mitchneck.pdf.

Malpas, J. E. *Place and Experience: A Philosophical Topography*. Cambridge: Cambridge University Press, 2007.

Manning, Paul. "The Hotel/Refugee Camp Iveria: Symptom, Monster, Fetish, Home." Paper presented at Trent University, November 2008.

———. "Materiality and Cosmology: Old Georgian Churches as Sacred, Sublime, and Secular Objects." *Ethnos* 73, no. 3 (2008) 1–34.

Massey, Douglas S., and Monica Espinoza Higgins. "The Effect of Immigration on Religious Belief and Practice: A Theologizing or Alienating Experience?" *Social Science Research*. 40, no. 5 (2011) 1371–89.

Matsuzato, Kimitaka. "Inter-Orthodox Relations and Transborder Nationalities in and around Unrecognised Abkhazia and Transnistria." *Religion, State and Society* 37, no. 3 (2009) 239–62.

Metcalf, Peter, and Richard Huntington. *Celebrations of Death : The Anthropology of Mortuary Ritual*. Cambridge: Cambridge University Press, 1991.

Meyendorff, John. *A Study of Gregory Palamas*. London: Faith, 1964.

Mundt, Alex, and Elizabeth Ferris. "Durable Solutions for IDPs in Protracted Situations: Three Case Studies." Paper presented at the ARC/Austcare Symposium, Canberra, Australia, October 28, 2008.

Nagy, Dorottya. *Migration and Theology: The Case of Chinese Christian Communities in Hungary and Romania in the Globalisation-Context*. Zoetermeer, Netherlands: Boekencentrum, 2009.

Nielsen, Anders. "Icons and Agency in the Georgian Orthodox Church." In *Religious Narrative, Cognition, and Culture: Image and Word in the Mind of Narrative*, edited by Armin W. Geertz and Jeppe Sinding Jensen, 219–36. Sheffield, UK: Equinox, 2011.

Ott, Craig, and Harold Netland. *Globalizing Theology: Belief and Practice in an Era of World Christianity*. Baker, 2006.

Ouspensky, Léonid. *Theology of the Icon*. Crestwood, NY: St. Vladimir's Seminary Press, 1978.

Ouspensky, Léonid, and Vladimir Lossky. *The Meaning of Icons*. Crestwood, NY: St. Vladimir's Seminary Press, 1982.

Owen, Elizabeth. "Georgia: Fence-Fight Continues with Russia, Separatists." *Eurasianet*, September 18, 2013. Accessed February 2015. http://www.eurasianet.org/node/67518.

Padilla, Elaine, and Peter C. Phan. *Contemporary Issues of Migration and Theology*. New York: Palgrave Macmillan, 2013.

Patriarch of Georgia. "International Charitable Foundation of The Catholicos-Patriarch of all Georgia Ilia II." Accessed April 9, 2014. http://patriarch.ge/eng/.

Pelkmans, Mathijs. *Conversion after Socialism: Disruptions, Modernisms and Technologies of Faith in the Former Soviet Union*. New York: Berghahn, 2009.

———. *Defending the Border: Identity, Religion, and Modernity in the Republic of Georgia*. Ithaca, NY: Cornell University Press, 2006.

Pipia, Oli. "Treasures of Georgia. Part 1. Temple of Ilory." *Steam Press*, September 16, 2012. Accessed September 27, 2017. https://www.streampress.com/news/multicultural/item/884-treasures-of-georgia-part-i-temple-of-ilory.html.

Priest, Robert J. "'Experience-Near Theologizing' in Diverse Human Contexts." In *Globalizing Theology: Belief and Practice in an Era of World Christianity*, edited by Craig Ott and Harold A. Netland, 180–95, Grand Rapids: Baker, 2006.

Quenot, Michel. *The Icon: Window on the Kingdom*. Crestwood, NY: St. Vladimir's Seminary, 1991.

Rapp, Stephen H., Jr. "Georgian Christianity." In *The Blackwell Companion to Eastern Christianity*, edited by Kenneth Parry, 138–55. Malden, MA: Blackwell, 2007.

Rosbrook, Bernadette, and Robert D. Schweitzer. "The Meaning of Home for Karen and Chin Refugees from Burma: An Interpretative Phenomenological Approach." *European Journal of Psychotherapy & Counselling* 12, no. 2 (2010) 159–72.

Roudometof, Victor, Alexander Agadjanian, and Jerry G Pankhurst. *Eastern Orthodoxy in a Global Age: Tradition Faces the Twenty-First Century*. Walnut Creek, CA: Alta Mira, 2005.

Rouner, Leroy S. *The Longing for Home*. Notre Dame: University of Notre Dame Press, 1996.

Rustaveli, Shota. *The Knight in the Panther's Skin: A Romantic Epic*. Tbilisi: Literatura Ka Khelovneba, 1966.

Scharen, Christian, and Anna Marie Vigen. *Ethnography as Christian Theology and Ethics*. Edited by C. Scharen and Anna Marie Vigen. London: Continuum, 2011.

Schlaeger, Jürgen, and Gesa Stedman. *Representations of Emotions*. Tübingen: Narr, 1999.

Schreiter, Robert J. *Constructing Local Theologies*. Maryknoll, NY: Orbis, 1985.

Schweitzer, Robert, and Zachary Steel. "Researching Refugees: Methodological and Ethical Cconsiderations." In *Doing CrossCultural Research: Ethical and Methodological Perspectives*, edited by Liamputtong Pranee, 87–101. Dordrecht: Springer, 2008.

Sedmak Clemens. *Doing Local Theology: A Guide for Artisans of a New Humanity*. Maryknoll, NY: Orbis, 2002.

Serrano, Silvia. "De-Secularizing National Space in Georgia." *Identity Studies* 2 (2010) 37–58. Accessed February 2015. http://ojs.iliauni.edu.ge/index.php/identitystudies/article/view/12/8.

Smith, Anthony D. *Chosen Peoples*. Oxford: Oxford University Press, 2003.

Smith, Jonathan A., and Mike Osborne. "Interpretative Phenomenological Analysis." In *Qualitative Psychology: A Practical Guide to Research Methods*, edited by Jonathan A. Smith, 53–80. London: Sage, 2008.

Smith, Jonathan A., Maria Jarman, and Mike Osborn. "Doing Interpretative Phenomenological Analysis." In *Qualitative Health Psychology: Theories and Methods*, edited by M. Murray and K. Chamberlain, 218–40. London: Sage, 1999.

Smith, Timothy Lawrence. *Religion and Ethnicity in America*. Washington, DC: American Historical Association, 1978.

Sulava, Ketevan. "At the Crossroads of Identity, Belonging and the Myth of Return: A Case Study of Georgian Internally Displaced Persons of 1992–93." *Conflict, Reconstruction and Human Security (CRS)*, 2010. http://hdl.handle.net/2105/8657.

Sunquist, Scott W., and Dale T. Irvin. *History of the World Christian Movement*. Vol 1. Maryknoll, NY: Orbis, 2001.

Suny, Ronald G. *The Making of the Georgian Nation.* Bloomington: Indiana University Press, 1994.

Tarkhan-Mouravi, George, and Nana Sumbadze. "The Abkhazian–Georgian Conflict And The Issue Of Internally Displaced Persons." *Innovation: The European Journal of Social Science Research* 19, no. 3–4 (2006) 283–302.

Taylor, Charles. *A Secular Age.* Cambridge, MA: Belknap, 2007.

Tsekhanskaia, Kira V. "The Icon in the Home: The Home Begins with the Icon." in *Religion and Politics in Russia: A Reader,* edited by Marjorie Mandelstam Balzer, 18–30. Armonk, NY: Sharpe, 2010.

Toumanoff, Cyrille. *Studies in Christian Caucasian History.* Washington, DC: Georgetown University Press, 1963.

Verdery, Katherine. *The Political Lives of Dead Bodies: Reburial and Postsocialist Change.* New York: Columbia University Press, 1999. http://ezproxy.asburyseminary.edu/login?url=http://search.ebscohost.com/login.aspx?direct=true&db=nlebk&AN=75805&site=eds-live.

Walker, Andrew Carras, Costa, ed. *Living Orthodoxy in the Modern World: Orthodox Christianity & Society.* Crestwood, NY: St. Vladimir's Seminary Press, 2000.

Weiss, Andrea "Crossing Conflicting State Boundaries: The Georgian-Abkhazian Ceasefire Line." In *Subverting Borders: Doing Research on Smuggling and Small-Scale Trade.* edited by Bettina Bruns and Judith Miggelbrink, 213–32. Wiesbaden: VS, 2012.

Index

Note: n indicates footnotes, and italicized page numbers indicate illustrations.

ABGEO, 33
Abkhazia, Georgia
   analysis, 13
   background and context of the Abkhazian Gali region, 43–44
   being led away from home, 75–76
   blurring the connection between biographies and place, 50–51
   borders and the reconciliation of place, 40, 42
   burial sites as places of national and religious imagination, 87
   collective grief of IDPs in displacement, 93–96
   conclusion, 119
   conflict and displacement, 27
   contested return to Gali, 45
   cross-border mission of Father Archil, 53
   displacement in the Georgian context, 17
   dynamics of border life, 44n12, 45
   at the edges of empires, 23
   establishing continuity with the past, 72, 74
   Georgian–Abkhazian War, 27–30
   graveyards and reimagining place, 83–84, 97–98

graveyards as sites of remembrance, 96–97
home and the remaking of lived lives, 63
home as a place of emotional longing, 65–66
home as a place of material abundance, 68–69
home as a place of nostalgic landscapes, 66
home as a place of relational authenticity, 69–70
Icon Corner as the sanctuary of the home, 78–79
icon returning to Ilory, 57–58, 61–62
"iconic" theology of home, 112–13
instrument, 10
introduction, xiii–xiv
locating Georgia, 20
loss of home as being between a resident and a tourist, 71
map of, 28
multiple displacements, 34
participants, 10
protracted displacement, 37
relations between Georgia and, 46–49
role of family and faith, 80

Index

Abkhazia, Georgia *(continued)*
  seeing things differently, 55–57
  Soviet religious policies and post-Soviet transitions, 23–24
  spiritual conditions of Gali, 53–54
  strategies of reconciling space, 55
  theological-social vision of icon and ecclesia, 109
Abkhazian Autonomous Republic, 23
Abkhazian War, 36
abundance, home as a place of, 68–72
Adams, Nicholas, 1
Administrative Border/Boundary Line (ABL)
  background and context of the Abkhazian Gali region, 43n6
  blurring the connection between biographies and place, 50n26
  borders and the reconciliation of place, 40–42
  contested return to Gali, 46
  dynamics of border life, 44–45
  establishing continuity with the past, 73
  icon returning to Ilory, 59n47
  map of, 42
Agadjanian, Alexander, 8
Agreement on a Ceasefire and Separation of Forces, 44
America, 70
analysis, 11–13
Anastasoios, Metropolitan, 9, 108
Anderson, Benedict, xvn5
Andrew the Apostle, 21
anthropology, Eastern Orthodox, 8–10
Apostles, the, 110
Archil, Father
  analysis, 13
  centrality of icons in Eastern Orthodox thought, 103
  cross-border mission of, 53
  at the edges of empires, 22
  home and the remaking of lived lives, 63
  icon returning to Ilory, 57–62
  iconic frame of borders, homes, and graves, 100
  invisible made visible, 109–10
  seeing things differently, 55–56
  spiritual conditions of Gali, 53–54
  strategies of reconciling space, 54–55
  theological-social vision of icon and ecclesia, 108
  theologizing the "iconic" borderland, 106–7
Armbruster, Heidi, 122
Armenia, 18, 20–22, 44n11
Armenian Apostolic Church, 20
Asia, 3, 18
ASSR (Autonomous Soviet Socialist Republic), 43
Atheistic Communism, 16–17, 24, 26, 56–57, 112
authenticity, home as a place of relational, 69–70
Autonomous Soviet Socialist Republic (ASSR), 43
Azerbaijan, 18, 44n11

background, theoretical, 5–10
background and context of the Abkhazian Gali region, 43–44
Balkan Wars, 31, 94
Bartholomew, Craig, 6
Basso, Keith, 5
Belarus, 44n11
Benz, Ernst, 101
Berdahl, Daphne, 52
between homes, 111–16
biographies and place, blurring the connection between, 50–52
Black Sea, 18, 21, 44, 53, 68
blurring the connection between biographies and place, 50–52
border life, dynamics of, 44–52
borderland, theologizing the "iconic," 106–11
borders, homes, and graves, iconic frame of, 99–118
borders and the reconciliation of place, 40–62
Bouchard, Michel, 85, 91n24, 92–93, 96–97
Bouma-Prediger, Steven, 14n38

Brezhnev, Leonid, 23
Brookings Institute, 31, 36
Brown, David, 108
Buga, 22
Bulgakov, Sergei, 109–10
burial sites as places of national and religious imagination, 85–87
Byzantium, Roman, 21

Casey, Edward, xv, 5, 7
Caspian Sea, 18
Catholicism, 8n23
Caucasia, 20, 22
Caucasus Barometer, 20
Caucasus Mountains, 18, 22, 23n19, 29–30, 40–41, 43
Caucasus Peace Forum, 33
Caucasus Research Resource Centers (CRRC), 25
Celebrations of Death (Metcalf and Huntington), 88
centrality of icons in Eastern Orthodox thought, 101–6
Chabukiani, Nana, 38n62
Charles, Robia, 25–26
Chechnya, Russia, 18
A Christian Theology of Place (Inge), 113
Chrysostom, John, 90
Chuberi, Georgia, 75
churches and lives, ruined, 53–54
CIS (Commonwealth of Independent States), 44
Clendenin, Daniel, 3
Clingerman, Forrest, 7n21
Coalition for Civil Society for Forced Migrants, 36
Cohen, Roberta, 29–31, 33
Colchis-Egrisi, Kingdom of, 20
collection, data, 10–11
collective grief, 93–96
Commission of Human Rights, 32
Commonwealth of Independent States (CIS), 44
Communism, Atheistic, 16–17, 24, 26, 56–57, 112
Communist Party, 43
Conciliation Resources, 33

conclusion, 119–22
conditions of Gali, spiritual, 53–54
conflict and displacement, 26–32
conflict between Georgia and Abkhazia, faces of, 46–49
connection between biographies and place, blurring the, 50–52
contact with the dead, visiting and maintaining, 90–93, *91*
contested return to Gali, 45–46
contested space, religious practice within, 52–54
context, displacement in the Georgian, 16–39
context and background of the Abkhazian Gali region, 43–44
continuity with the past, establishing, 72–74
Conversion of Kartli, 23
Corso, Molly, 83
Creet, Julia, 66
cross-border mission of Father Archil, 53
Crow, Gillian, 107
CRRC (Caucasus Research Resource Centers), 25
Cruz, Gemma Tulud, 3–4, 121

Dagestan, Russia, 18
Dalmais, Irénée, 110
data collection, 10–11
death, Georgian Orthodox views on, 88–93, *91*
defining home, 64
delimitations, 13–14
Deng, Francis M., 29–33
despair, loss of home leading to feelings of, 67–68
differently, seeing things, 55–57
displaced gaze, the, 119–22
displacement(s)
  collective grief of IDPs in, 93–96
  conflict and, 26–32
  faith narratives in, 74–82
  in the Georgian context, 16–39
  internal, 30–34
  multiple, 34–36
  place and, 5–8

displacement(s) *(continued)*
  places of, 40–98
  protracted, 36–38
  remaking home in, 72–74, 80–82
  theology in the context of, 99–118
Ditsi, Georgia, 51
Dixazurga, Gali, 73
Dunn, Elizabeth Cullen, 35n53
dynamics of border life, 44–52
dynamics of Georgian IDPs, 32–38

Easter, xiv, 13, 83–84, 90
Eastern Europe, 4
The Eastern Orthodox Church: Its Thought and Life (Benz), 101
ecclesia, theological-social vision of icon and, 108–9
edges of empires, at the, 20–23
Elliott, Charles, 1
emotional longing, home as a place of, 65–66
empires, at the edges of, 20–23
Enguri Border, 73
Enguri Bridge, 44, 87
Enguri River, 27, 28, 43n6, 44
establishing and maintaining relationship in mourning rituals, 88–89
establishing continuity with the past, 72–74
Eurasia, 18
Europe, 4, 18, 31, 85
Evdokimov, Paul, 108

faces of conflict between Georgia and Abkhazia, 46–49
faith and family, role of, 80–82
faith narratives in displacement, 74–82
family and faith, role of, 80–82
Fiddes, Paul, 1n2
Florensky, Pavel, 104–5
Forced Migration Online (FMO), 30
Forrest, Jim, 120
frame, theologizing the place of graves in the iconic, 116–18
frame of borders, homes, and graves, iconic, 99–118
Frichova, Magdalena, 33, 49

fulfillment, home as the provision of psychological, 64–68

Gabriel, 81
Gali
  background and context of the Abkhazian Gali region, 43–44
  blurring the connection between biographies and place, 50–52
  borders and the reconciliation of place, 40–42
  conclusion, 119
  contested return to, 45–46
  cross-border mission of Father Archil, 53
  dynamics of border life, 44–45
  establishing continuity with the past, 73n26, 74
  Georgian–Abkhazian relations, 46, 48
  home as a place of emotional longing, 65
  home as a place of material abundance, 68
  icon returning to Ilory, 58–59, 62
  map of, 42
  religious practice within contested spaces, 52
  seeing things differently, 55–56
  spiritual conditions of, 53–54
  split between Georgian IDPs and returnees, 49–50
  strategies of reconciling space, 55
  theologizing the "iconic" borderland, 106
Gap Analysis, UNHCR, 34
gaze, the displaced, 119–22
Geneva Peace Process, 44
George of Ilory, St., 57–59
Georgian National Guard, 27
Georgian–Abkhazian War, 17, 26–30, 37, 43, 75
Gerliani, Ramaz, 36
Germany, 52
God
  analysis, 12
  being led away from home, 75–76

centrality of icons in Eastern Orthodox thought, 101–3
conclusion, 119–20
Eastern Orthodox anthropology, 9–10
Eastern Orthodox theology, 2–3
hiddenness and visibility of home and, 114–16
home and the remaking of lived lives, 64
Icon Corner as the sanctuary of the home, 77
icon returning to Ilory, 59–60
iconic frame of borders, homes, and graves, 100
"iconic" theology of home, 111–14
instrument, 11
introduction, xiv–xv
invisible made visible, 109–10
methodology, 2
place and displacement, 6, 7n21
role of family and faith, 80
spiritual conditions of Gali, 54
theological-social vision of icon and ecclesia, 108–9
theologizing the "iconic" borderland, 106
theologizing the place of graves in the iconic frame, 117
Goltz, Hermann, 3
grave relations, 90–93, 91
graves, borders, and homes, iconic frame of, 99–118
graves in the iconic frame, theologizing the place of, 116–18
graveyards and reimagining place, 83–98
Greek Empire, 20
Gregory the Illuminator, St., 21
grief, collective, 93–96
Groody, Daniel, 121
The Guiding Principles on Internal Displacement, 32

Hanganu, Gabriel, 9, 59–60
Hann, Chris, 3
A Heavy Burden (Lois and Tavartkiladze), 38, 46

Hewitt, George, 29
hiddenness and visibility of God and home, 114–16
Higgins, Monica, xiiin2
Holocaust, 85
Holy Spirit, 108
home
  being led away from, 75–76
  defining, 64
  Icon Corner as the sanctuary of the, 77–80, 78
  "iconic" theology of, 111–16
  loss of as being between a resident and a tourist, 71–72
  loss of leading to feelings of despair, 67–68
  as a place of abundance, 68–72
  as a place of emotional longing, 65–66
  as a place of nostalgic landscapes, 66–67
  as a place of relational authenticity, 69–70
  as the provision of psychological fulfillment, 64–68
  as the re-creation of sacred spaces, 76–82
  remaking in displacement, 72–74, 80–82
  and the remaking of lived lives, 63–82
homes, graves, and borders, iconic frame of, 99–118
Hotel Iveria, 35
"How Dynamic is the Structure of Employment and Well-being," 81
Human Rights Watch, 45
Huntington, Richard, 88

IASFM (International Association for the Study of Forced Migration), 30n38
icon and ecclesia, theological-social vision of, 108–9
Icon Corner as the sanctuary of the home, 77–80, 78
icon returning to Ilory, 57–62

"iconic" borderland, theologizing the, 106–11
iconic frame of borders, homes, and graves, 99–118
iconic frame, theologizing the place of graves in the, 116–18
"iconic" theology of home, 111–16
icons in Eastern Orthodox thought, centrality of, 101–6
IDPs (Internally Displaced Persons)
　collective grief of in displacement, 93–96
　dynamics of Georgian, 32–38
　split between returnees and Georgian, 49–50
　understanding religious aspects of Georgian, 38–39
Ilia II, Patriarch, 24–25, 85
Ilory Church, 24, 57–62, 63, 108–9
imagination, burial sites as places of national and religious, 85–87
importance of study, 14–15
Incarnation of Jesus, 9, 100–103, 108
Indonesia, 18
Inge, John, 3, 6, 113
Ingram, Anne, 90n20, 93
Ingushetia, Russia, 18
instrument, 10–11
integration and isolation, between, 33–34
An Intercultural Theology of Migration: Pilgrims in the Wilderness (Cruz), 3
internal displacement, 30–34
International Association for the Study of Forced Migration (IASFM), 30n38
International Centre on Conflicts and Negotiation, 25
International Charitable Foundation of the Catholicos-Patriarch of all Georgia, 24–25
Internet, 70
Interpretative Phenomenological Analysis (IPA), 11–12
introduction, xiii–xvi
invisible made visible, 109–11
Iskander, Fazil, 86–87

Islam
　borders and the reconciliation of place, 41
　at the edges of empires, 22
　Icon Corner as the sanctuary of the home, 79
　"iconic" theology of home, 112
　locating Georgia, 18, 20
　seeing things differently, 56
　spiritual conditions of Gali, 54
isolation and integration, between, 33–34

Jacob, 104
Jarman, Maria, 11
Jesus Christ
　centrality of icons in Eastern Orthodox thought, 101–3
　Eastern Orthodox anthropology, 9
　iconic frame of borders, homes, and graves, 100
　introduction, xiv
　invisible made visible, 109–10
　theological-social vision of icon and ecclesia, 108
　theologizing the place of graves in the iconic frame, 117
　visiting and maintaining contact with the dead, 90
John of Damascus, St., 101–2
Joseph, 94

Kabachnik, Peter, 27, 37–38, 52, 71, 98
Kabardino-Balkaria, Russia, 18
Kamani, Abkhazia, 24
Karachevo-Cherkessia, Russia, 18
Kartli-Iberia, Kingdom of, 20–22
Kazakhstan, 44n11
Kazbegi, Georgia, 91
Khomushkuri, Georgia, 46
King, Charles, 28–29, 41
The Knight in the Panther Skin, 18
Kotthoff, Helga, 89–90, 95
Kutaisi, Georgia, 33
Kyrgyzstan, 44n11

landscapes, home as a place of nostalgic, 66–67
Lane, Belden, 67
Larson-Miller, Lizette, 88
Lawrence-Zúñiga, Denise, 48, 97
led away from home, being, 75–76
Lester, Andrew, 76
lives, home and the remaking of lived, 63–82
lives, ruined churches and, 53–54
Lives of the Georgian Saints (Machitadze), 58
living and dead, maintaining relationship between, 88–93, *91*
Living in Limbo, 45
locating Georgia, 17–26
Lois, Anne-Sophie, 38–39
longing, home as a place of emotional, 65–66
Lord's Prayer, 75
loss of home
  as being between a resident and a tourist, 71–72
  leading to feelings of despair, 67–68
Lossky, Vladimir, 103
Louth, Andrew, 103, 105, 111
Low, Setha, 48, 97

Machitadze, Zakaria, 58
Mafia, 47
maintaining relationship between living and dead, 88–93, *91*
Malpas, Jeff, 6, 14
Manning, Paul, 24
maps of Georgia, *19*
Masses in Flight (Cohen and Deng), 30, 32
Massey, Douglas, xiiin2
material abundance, home as a place of, 68–69
Metcalf, Peter, 88
methodology, 1–15
Middle East, 18
Migration and Theology, The Case of Chinese Christian Communities in Hungary and Romania and the Globalisation-Context (Nagy), 4

mission of Father Archil, cross-border, 53
Mitchneck, Beth, 34n52
Mkheidze, Prince Constantine, 22
Mkheidze, Prince David, 22
Moldova, 44n11
Moscow, Russia, 28, 53, 69–70, 93
Moscow Agreement, 44
Moses, 93
mourning rituals, establishing and maintaining relationship in, 88–89
Muhammad, Marwan ibn, 22
multiple displacements, 34–36

Nagy, Dorottya, 4, 121
narratives in displacement, faith, 74–82
national and religious imagination, burial sites as places of, 85–87
National Science Foundation, 81
National Statistics Office of Georgia, 20
Nauru, 45
Neo-Platonism, 18
New Testament, 6, 102
Nicaragua, 45
Nicolas, St., 82, 115, 120
Nielsen, Anders, 10, 77
Nino, St., 21
North Caucasus, 18, 29
North Ossetia, Russia, 18
Norwegian Refugee Council (NRC), 39
nostalgic landscapes, home as a place of, 66–67

Ochamchire, Abkhazia, 57, 70–71, 78–79
Office for Religious Affairs, Georgian, 23
Old Testament, 6, 102
"On the Cemetery's Name and the Cross" (Chrysostom), 90
oppression, Soviet religious, 23–26
Orthodox Church of Georgia, 23–27, 53, 55, 57n42
Osborne, Mike, 11–12

Ossetian War, 17, 36
Ottoman Empire, 20, 56, 112
Ouspensky, Leonid, 101–2

participants, 10
past, establishing continuity with the, 72–74
Pekaliani, David, 74
Pelkmans, Mathijs, 51n29
Persia, 21
Persian Empire, 20–21
Pityus, 21
place(s)
  of abundance, home as a, 68–72
  blurring the connection between biographies and, 50–52
  and displacement, 5–8
  of displacement, 40–98
  of emotional longing, home as a, 65–66
  of graves in the iconic frame, theologizing the, 116–18
  graveyards and reimagining, 83–98
  of national and religious imagination, burial sites as, 85–87
  of nostalgic landscapes, home as, 66–67
  of relational authenticity, home as, 69–70
"Places of Experience and the Experience of Place" (Platt), 64
Platt, Katherine, 64, 79
policies, Soviet religious, 23–26
The Political Lives of Dead Bodies (Verdery), 94
Pontus, Kingdom of, 20
Portugal, 65–66, 70
practice within contested space, religious, 52–54
Priest, Robert, 2n5
procedure, 11
Protestantism, 8n23, 14
protracted displacement, 36–38
provision of psychological fulfillment, home as the, 64–68
psychological fulfillment, home as the provision of, 64–68

Quadripartite Agreement on Voluntary Return of Refugees and Displaced Persons, 44n12, 45–46
Quenot, Michel, 104

Racha, Georgia, 20
Rapp, Stephen, 21–23
reconciliation of place, borders and the, 40–62
reconciling space, strategies of, 54–62
re-creation of sacred spaces, home as the, 76–82
Red Cross, xiv
Refugee Study Center, 30
regions of Georgia, *19*
reimagining place, graveyards and, 83–98
relational authenticity, home as a place of, 69–70
relations, Georgian–Abkhazian, 46–49
relations, grave, 90–93, *91*
relationship between living and dead, maintaining, 88–93, *91*
religious and national imagination, burial sites as places of, 85–87
religious aspects of Georgian IDPs, understanding, 38–39
religious policies, oppression, and renewal, Soviet, 23–26
religious practice within contested spaces, 52–54
remaking home in displacement, 72–74, 80–82
remaking of lived lives, home and the, 63–82
remembrance, graveyards as sites of, 96–97
renewal, Soviet religious, 23–26
Republic Square, 35
resident and tourist, loss of home as being between a, 71–72
return and settlement, between, 36–38
return to Gali, contested, 45–46
returnees and IDPs, split between Georgian, 49–50
returning to Ilory, icon, 57–62

rituals, establishing and maintaining relationship in mourning, 88–89
role of family and faith, 80–82
Roman Empire, 20–21
Rome, 21
Roudometof, Victor, 8
ruined churches and lives, 53–54
Russia
    collective grief of IDPs in displacement, 93
    displacement in the Georgian context, 17
    dynamics of border life, 44–45
    at the edges of empires, 20
    establishing continuity with the past, 72
    home as a place of material abundance, 68
    Icon Corner as the sanctuary of the home, 77
    locating Georgia, 18
    seeing things differently, 56–57
    Soviet religious policies and post-Soviet transitions, 24
Russian Orthodox Church, 101
Rustaveli, Shota, 18
Rustavi, Georgia, 10, 93

sacred spaces, home as the re-creation of, 76–82
Salvation Army, 11n32
Samegrelo, Georgia, 20
sanctuary of the home, Icon Corner as the, 77–80, 78
Saroyan, 43
Sarpi, Georgia, 51n29
Scharen, Christian, 1
Schweitzer, Robert, 11
Scorpions, the, 48
seeing things differently, 55–57
Serrano, Sylvia, 61
settlement and return, between, 36–38
Shevardnadze, Edward, 29n34
Smith, Anthony, 85
Smith, Jonathan, 11–12
Smith, Timothy, xiiin2
Social Programs Foundation, 71

social-theological vision of icon and ecclesia, 108–9
Sokhumi, Georgia
    being led away from home, 75
    burial sites as places of national and religious imagination, 87
    collective grief of IDPs in displacement, 95
    contested return to Gali, 46
    dynamics of border life, 44
    establishing continuity with the past, 74
    Georgian–Abkhazian War, 27–29
    hiddenness and visibility of God and home, 114
    home as a place of emotional longing, 65–66
    home as a place of material abundance, 68
    home as a place of nostalgic landscapes, 67
    Icon Corner as the sanctuary of the home, 78
    icon returning to Ilory, 58
    introduction, xiii
    loss of home as being between a resident and a tourist, 71
    loss of home leading to feelings of despair, 67–68
    protracted displacement, 37
    split between Georgian IDPs and returnees, 49
Somalia, 31
South Caucasus, 18, 20, 22
South Ossetia, Georgia, 20, 51
Soviet rule, Georgia under
    background and context of the Abkhazian Gali region, 43
    displacement in the Georgian context, 16–17
    dynamics of border life, 44n11, 44n14
    at the edges of empires, 20, 23
    Georgian–Abkhazian War, 27–30
    home as a place of material abundance, 68
    icon returning to Ilory, 61
    multiple displacements, 35

Soviet rule, Georgia under *(continued)*
  religious policies and transitions after, 23–26
  religious practice within contested spaces, 52
  spiritual conditions of Gali, 54
Soviet Union
  background and context of the Abkhazian Gali region, 43
  burial sites as places of national and religious imagination, 86
  displacement in the Georgian context, 17
  Georgian–Abkhazian War, 28, 30
  home as a place of material abundance, 68
  Soviet religious policies and post-Soviet transitions, 24
  spiritual conditions of Gali, 53
space, religious practice within contested, 52–54
space, strategies of reconciling, 54–62
spaces, home as the re-creation of sacred, 76–82
spiritual conditions of Gali, 53–54
split between Georgian IDPs and returnees, 49–50
St. George of Ilory, 57–59
St. Gregory the Illuminator, 21
St. John of Damascus, 101–2
St. Nicolas, 82, 115, 120
St. Nino, 21
Stalin, Joseph, 27
Steel, Zachary, 11
Stepansminda, Georgia, 91
strategies of reconciling space, 54–62
study, importance of, 14–15
Sudan, 31
Sulava, Ketevan, 37–38, 98
Suny, Ronald, 20–21
Svaneti, Georgia, 20, 75

Tajikistan, 44n11
Tavartkiladze, Tamar, 38–39
Taylor, Charles, xvn5
Tbilisi, Georgia
  being led away from home, 75
  blurring the connection between biographies and place, 51n28
  burial sites as places of national and religious imagination, 87
  collective grief of IDPs in displacement, 93
  contested return to Gali, 46
  cross-border mission of Father Archil, 53
  delimitations, 14
  displacement in the Georgian context, 16
  dynamics of border life, 44–45
  at the edges of empires, 22
  Georgian–Abkhazian relations, 47–48
  Georgian–Abkhazian War, 27–29
  home as a place of nostalgic landscapes, 67
  Icon Corner as the sanctuary of the home, 78–79
  internal displacement, 33
  introduction, xiv
  loss of home as being between a resident and a tourist, 72
  loss of home leading to feelings of despair, 68
  multiple displacements, 35–36
  participants, 10
  procedure, 11
  protracted displacement, 37
  role of family and faith, 80–81
  Soviet religious policies and post-Soviet transitions, 25
Theodorou, Maria, 35
theology
  in the context of displacement, 99–118
  Eastern Orthodox, 2–4
  of home, "iconic," 111–16
  in the "iconic" borderland, 106–11
  and the place of graves in the iconic frame, 116–18
  vision of icon and ecclesia in the context of sociology and, 108–9
theoretical background, 5–10
thought, centrality of icons in Eastern Orthodox, 101–6

Three Treatises on the Divine Images
(St. John), 101
tourist and resident, loss of home as being between a, 71–72
transitions after Soviet rule, 23–26
Trebizond, 21
Trinity, 101, 110
Trinity Cathedral, 53
Tsekhanskaia, Kira, 77
Tserovani, 73
Tshuguaanis, 89
Tshuguashivilis, 89
Tungia, Tangizi, 57
Turkey, 18
Turkmenistan, 44n11
Tuvalu, 45

Ukraine, 24, 44n11
understanding religious aspects of Georgian IDPs, 38–39
UNHCR (United Nations High Commissioner for Refugees), 34, 36, 44n12
United Nations, 31, 39, 55–56
University of Oxford, 30
Uzbekistan, 44n11

Vanuatu, 45
Vardosanidze, Sergo, 23
Venezuela, 45
Verdery, Katherine, 94
views on death, Georgian Orthodox, 88–93, *91*
Vigen, Anna, 1
Virgin Mary, 103
visibility and hiddenness of God and home, 114–16
visible, invisible made, 109–11
vision of icon and ecclesia, theological-social, 108–9
visiting and maintaining contact with the dead, 90–93, *91*

Wahabbism, 54
Walsh, Brian, 14n38
Wardrop, Marjory, 18
Weiss, Andrea, 43
West Caucasus, 44
Wiesel, Eli, 66
World War II, 31, 85

Zugdidi, Georgia, 33, 40, 50n26, 51, 59, 79

www.ingramcontent.com/pod-product-compliance
Lightning Source LLC
Chambersburg PA
CBHW051941160426
43198CB00013B/2252